The Secret of
INSTANT
HEALING

OTHER HAY HOUSE TITLES
BY DR. FRANK J. KINSLOW

The Secret of Quantum Living
(available January 2012)

Eufeeling! The Art of Creating
Inner Peace and Outer Prosperity
(available July 2012)

Beyond Happiness: How You Can
Fulfill Your Deepest Desire
(available January 2013)

All of the above are available at your local bookstore,
or may be ordered by visiting:

Hay House USA: **www.hayhouse.com**®
Hay House Australia: **www.hayhouse.com.au**
Hay House UK: **www.hayhouse.co.uk**
Hay House South Africa: **www.hayhouse.co.za**
Hay House India: **www.hayhouse.co.in**

The Secret of

INSTANT HEALING

Dr. Frank J. Kinslow

HAY HOUSE, INC.
Carlsbad, California • New York City
London • Sydney • Johannesburg
Vancouver • Hong Kong • New Delhi

Published and distributed in the United States by: Hay House, Inc.: www
.hayhouse.com • **Published and distributed in Australia by:** Hay House Australia Pty. Ltd.: www.hayhouse.com.au • **Published and distributed in the
United Kingdom by:** Hay House UK, Ltd.: www.hayhouse.co.uk • **Published
and distributed in the Republic of South Africa by:** Hay House SA (Pty), Ltd.:
www.hayhouse.co.za • **Distributed in Canada by:** Raincoast: www.raincoast
.com • **Published in India by:** Hay House Publishers India: www.hayhouse
.co.in

Project editor: Lisa Mitchell • *Cover design:* Julie Davison • *Interior design:*
Nick C. Welch • *Interior illustrations:* Courtesy of the author

Quantum Entrainment® is a registered trademark of Dr. Frank J. Kinslow.

First published in 2008 by TRIAD Publishing Group, ISBN: 978-0-9815045-1-
3; and also by Lucid Sea, LLC, ISBN: 978-0-6152268-0-4.

Library of Congress Cataloging-in-Publication Data

Kinslow, Frank J.
  The secret of instant healing / Frank J Kinslow.
     p. cm.
   ISBN 978-1-4019-3194-0 (pbk.)
 1. Health. 2. Awareness. 3. Mind and body. I. Title.
 RA776.5.K48 2011
 613--dc22

                                        2011000877

Tradepaper ISBN: 978-1-4019-3194-0
Digital ISBN: 978-1-4019-3195-7

14 13 12 11   4 3 2 1
1st Hay House edition, June 2011

FSC
www.fsc.org
MIX
Packaging from
responsible sources
FSC® C008955

Printed in the United States of America

In memory of my Mom,
my lifelong friend.

CONTENTS

PREFACE

What if I told you that just by being aware of a problem you could fix it?

"Sure," you say. "I become aware of a problem and then I take steps to correct it. What's so special about that?"

This is pretty much the way life unfolds, isn't it? But that's not what I'm talking about. What if you just become aware of a problem and, with no more effort on your part, *awareness* did the fixing? Would that be special? Sure it would. And that's exactly what I am talking about. If you become aware of an arthritic knee, indigestion, a headache, anger or fear, a failing relationship, or the loss of a job in just the right way, the organizing genius of awareness will fix what is broken. That is not just special—it is a wonderment. It is a skill that could alter your life, and the planet, in unimaginable ways.

This is a method of embracing life that would soften and enliven the world we live in, transforming it into the world of our dreams. Simply put, becoming aware of the healing and organizing force of awareness is the answer to the problems that have plagued us since we first stood erect and stepped headlong into the human condition.

If it seems as if I have overinflated the role of awareness in attuning your life to your inherent wisdom, I have not. And it will only take you a few minutes to discover the accuracy of my assertion. This is a small book wielding stupendous potential. But you don't have to take my word for it—not at all. What I am offering you is a scientifically reproducible process that anyone can do. All you need is awareness.

Are you aware? Are you conscious of reading these words? Do you know if you are sitting or standing? Do you know what you are thinking right now? Then that settles it. You can learn the simple steps that refine your awareness and heal your body and mind. You can also learn to heal the bodies and minds of others. And, with a little help from your friends, you are poised to transmute the ills of humankind on this Earth.

Are you ready? Do you feel a sense of anticipation, a feeling of imminent discovery? What is revealed to you within the pages of this simple book will be your private journey. You will know its impact by the deeds you perform once you've read it. The rest is easy. You only have to turn the page to forever change your life.

CHAPTER 1

BEGINNING

*"Anything will give up its secrets if you love it enough. . . .
I have found that when I silently commune with people
they give up their secrets also—if you love them enough."*

— GEORGE WASHINGTON CARVER

There is a subtle secret waiting for you, closer than your next breath, more vital than your next heartbeat. Once you grasp it, your life will open up to wonders light-years beyond what you thought possible. It is the key to health, joy, and peace; and it is working right now as you read these lines. But this secret is hidden from you, not within the symbols of an obscure parchment kept deep in the bowels of an ancient temple, but right before your very eyes.

This book will reveal that secret and show you how to draw from its depths to enrich your life and the lives of your family, friends, and even your pets. In the pages that follow, you will learn how to heal body, mind, and soul as effortlessly as watching a sunset. The scientific procedure that will unfold before you is easily learned and readily applied by all. It is as simple as the secret itself, and just as powerful.

I recommend that you do not jump ahead, but read this book page by page. It is in this way that the secret will find its home in your consciousness. Please take time to do each exercise as it is presented. You will be learning a new skill, and some practice is necessary for it to become second nature. The exercises are not difficult—in fact, they are delightful, nurturing, and enlivening. So no matter how eager you are to start working wonders, take your time on the basics. As a wise teacher once shared, "Well begun is half done."

On your trek, you will first gain an understanding of what awareness is and where it can be found. Then you will meet the secret face-to-face and embrace it as an old friend. Finally, you will learn how to use it to heal your body, harmonize your emotions, and sharpen your mind in order to create a more productive and joyful life. Of course, you will be able to share your knowledge with others, healing and enlivening their lives as well.

This secret is hidden from you, not within the symbols of an obscure parchment kept deep in the bowels of an ancient temple, but right before your very eyes.

CHAPTER 2

THE SECRET REVEALED

"The ultimate value of life depends upon awareness and the power of contemplation rather than upon mere survival."

— ARISTOTLE

I would like to ask you a simple question. Understanding the answer could change your life forever, so think it through thoroughly and then continue reading. Here is the question: *What is most important to you in this life?*

What did you come up with? Health? Family? Mind? Job? Ice cream? My answer to this question is *awareness*. Without awareness, you have nothing. You cannot love your spouse and children, work at your job, or sip coffee at a sidewalk café without it. For all intents and purposes, without awareness you do not exist.

Awareness is not your mind. If your mind were a light-bulb, then awareness would be the electricity that lights it up. A dull reflection of awareness in the mind causes confusion, misunderstanding, and ultimately, suffering. A mind bright with awareness is calm and present. It displays a peaceful gentleness that puts others at ease. If you look at awareness as your "inner light," you will be close to understanding its vital importance.

The quality of your awareness determines the quality of your life. It is crucial that your awareness be vibrant and awake. Let's say that you are sitting in a completely dark room next to a window. It is predawn, but light is just starting to enter the room when you look down and see an unidentifiable form at your feet. Fascinated, you continue to watch as, little by little, the room lightens and you begin to see the object more clearly.

All at once and to your horror, you realize that the object is a coiled snake ready to strike. You are immobilized by fear. Your mind is firing off frantic thoughts: *Is the snake poisonous? If I move a muscle, will it strike? How will I get help if I'm bitten?* You sit stone still as the light continues to slowly illuminate the room and note that for some reason the snake has not yet struck. You begin to relax and think more clearly. Your mind quickly reviews escape scenarios while your body remains rigid and unmoving. The sun crests the horizon, and the first rays of dawn break through the window, filling the room with a delicate golden light. Then, like the brightness of lightning on the blackness of night, you see that the snake is actually a coiled rope.

You felt fear. Your mind froze and then shattered, thoughts scattered like broken glass. All the while your tense body was pumping stress hormones into your blood, preparing you for battle. In those few moments, you may have aged months. Why? Simply because you perceived a threat where there was none.

> *The quality of your awareness determines the quality of your life.*

We can equate the darkness with impaired awareness. Overwork, lack of exercise, drugs, alcohol, poor diet, anger, greed, and grief all dampen consciousness and impair our ability to view the world in a nonthreatening way.

Our lives are filled with perceived threats. We have financial snakes, job snakes, family snakes, and so on. Even while driving to a pleasant event such as a movie or the beach, a traffic jam can ruin the mood, leading to soaring blood pressure and exploding tempers. We are the *fight-or-flight* generation perceiving snakes around every corner.

How do we change those perceptions? How do we enjoy the full light of day, exposing those snakes for the ineffectual ropes that they are? Well, we simply become more aware. Awareness is like sunlight. It lightens the emotions and enlightens the mind. Dull minds and muddy emotions are poor reflectors of awareness. Perception is fueled by our awareness. Pure awareness can never be fooled by a rope.

We are the "fight-or-flight" generation perceiving snakes around every corner.

Most of the time our minds are on autopilot. Incessant mental chatter is a good example of runaway thoughts. The hyperactive brain—so common today that it's considered normal—wastes vast amounts of energy and continually gets us into trouble. Other symptoms include worrying about the future or dwelling on the past; and feeling bored, frustrated, angry, anxious, or fearful. These are all ropes that look like snakes. Dull awareness makes our world a scary place.

Awareness is everywhere all the time, but we just don't pay attention to it. I know that might sound weird, but it's true. Normally we are preoccupied with the people, thoughts, and "stuff" that make up our everyday lives. We are aware of those things, but are we aware of awareness? Not often. Most of us wouldn't know pure awareness if it walked right up and shook our hand . . . but that is about to change.

Awareness is everywhere all the time,
but we just don't pay attention to it.

Wait a minute. That's it? That's the secret? Awareness?! You're probably feeling a little disappointed right now. I would too if I thought that I could own the secret to the universe simply by identifying what happens when it's in short supply. You may not have a very clear idea of what I'm talking about, either. That is because pure awareness can't be captured in the mind's eye. You can't take a picture of it. Awareness is not a thing, idea, or emotion. So talking about it can be frustrating if you want to own it with your mind. It's not physical; you can't grab hold of awareness and use it like a hammer. However, once you have experienced—or actually, "non-experienced"—pure awareness directly, all this will make perfect and beautiful sense.

If you're confused at this point, don't worry. You do not have to understand anything about awareness to make it work wonders in your life. That said, it will be valuable to have some knowledge about it to explain to others why they can feel so good, so fast. As you will soon discover, you will be creating miracles and having fun. Pure awareness will be as natural to you as breathing.

Okay, are you ready for a little book learnin'? Good.

You do not have to understand anything about
awareness to make it work wonders in your life.

CHAPTER 3

AWARENESS AND THE UNIVERSE

"The moment one gives close attention to anything, even a blade of grass, it becomes a mysterious, awesome, indescribably magnificent world in itself."

— HENRY MILLER

Turn the page and take a look at Figure 1: The Material Model. Start by noting the horizontal line near the bottom, which represents the division between the phenomenal world of created things and the "no-thing" from which they were created. Above is the infinity of creation and below the unbounded abode of pure awareness.

Pure awareness is without form—meaning it has no boundaries that our minds can identify. Our minds, the containers for our thoughts and emotions, work with things that can be recognized by their differing forms. Through our senses we are kept in contact with the material world. We can distinguish a bagel from a bullfrog by their differences. This may seem rather simplistic; but our brain's job is to identify various forms, label and categorize them, and then use them or file them for future use.

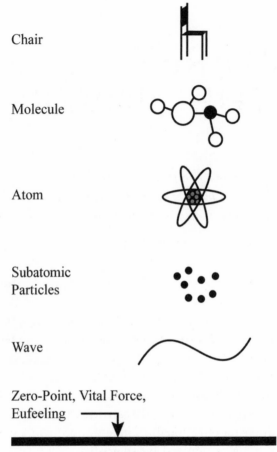

Chair

Molecule

Atom

Subatomic
Particles

Wave

Zero-Point, Vital Force,
Eufeeling

Pure Awareness
No Energy, Nothing, No Form, Non-Experience

Figure 1: The Material Model

This whole process is accomplished by a thought, which is a form. Thoughts and emotions are mental forms. Ideas, beliefs, hopes, and philosophies are an assemblage of thoughts around a central theme much as a chair is an assemblage of molecules around the idea of supporting you in a sitting position. Thoughts are not as tangible as material objects, but they are objects, nonetheless. The point is that all things in the universe are individual and unique. Each object is separated and identified by its unique form.

Below the horizontal line in the figure, you can find that pure awareness has no form. Think of it as the blank page on which the words are to be written. Awareness is formless, unbounded, undifferentiated, and pure. It is one without a second. Because pure awareness is formless, it cannot be recognized by your mind. No matter how hard you try, you won't be able to understand awareness. Neither will you be able to control or manipulate it. It doesn't exist as a thing, so as far as your mind is concerned, it does not exist—but it *does*.

So here is the task we have ahead of us. We must find something with no form or substance. Then we must come to know this *no-thing* more intimately than we know our own mind. Finally, we must use this unusable non-force to heal ourselves and others.

Are you beginning to realize why this knowledge is secret? This secret exists because we live in our mind, unaware of awareness. Despite a lifetime of experience to the contrary, we believe our mind when it tells us that lasting joy, peace, and love come from things. We fall for that old trick time and time again. And we believe our mind when it tells us that nothing has no value. But it does.

> *Despite a lifetime of experience to the contrary,*
> *we believe our mind when it tells us that lasting*
> *joy, peace, and love come from things.*

Pure awareness has no boundaries, so there is nothing that can change about awareness. That kind of nothing lasts forever. All other things, which means all of creation, change and eventually cease existing. Change is the only constant in the created realm. The instant a thing is created, it begins its journey to extinction. Pure awareness never changes or dies. It is the field of undying love and unbounded peace.

Now here's the kicker. Everything that has form comes out of formless pure awareness. Don't ask me how; it just does. Out of the womb of pure awareness is spun the web of creation. Quantum physics has discovered the realm of pure awareness, theoretically at least. David Bohm, one of the foremost theoretical physicists of his generation, identified an *unbounded whole* in which an implicate order is contained. This is not to be confused with the zero-point field or quantum state, which is the lowest energy state of a particle or object. What Bohm referred to has no energy. Plainly stated, this field contains the *stuff* of creation silently waiting to become form or energy. So what Bohm was telling us is that everything comes from nothing. He taught that—and I'm making a bit of an inductive leap here—creation springs out of the nothing of pure awareness. You will actually experience this later when you learn how to stop your thinking, then watch your thoughts materialize again out of nothing. Now let's turn our eyes back toward the phenomenal creation found above the horizontal line.

Everything in creation expresses two qualities: order and energy. Let's use the chair you are sitting on to demonstrate this point. What you call your chair is actually energy in the form of a chair. We know it exhibits energy because your chair keeps your derriere in the air. (I love poetry, don't you?) Order, in the energy-order equation, is expressed by the form of your chair. So it doesn't matter if we are referring to stars or atoms, amoebae or zebras; everything is energy and form.

Out of the womb of pure awareness is
spun the web of creation.

The most basic created form is the wave. Just before the wave, and just after pure awareness on the creation hierarchy, you will find the zero-point field or quantum state. I add this tidbit for those who are familiar with quantum theory and want to appreciate my position more fully. If you are oriented toward the healing sciences, however, this most basic level of creation is often referred to as the vital force: that which breathes life into organic existence. A wave is infinite, stretching out endlessly. Where waves overlap they create subatomic particles. When the particles become more compact, they become atoms. Atoms huddle together to form molecules, and molecules arrange themselves in physical forms such as chairs, flowers, and cars.

Everything in creation expresses two qualities:
order and energy.

In our energy-order hierarchy, the more tangible the order of a thing is the less energy it expresses. Your chair is pretty solid compared to a subatomic particle. Subatomic particles are slippery little guys. If you know the exact location of one, you still don't know how fast or in what direction it's moving. Likewise, if you clock its exact speed, you won't be able to find it. My children were like adolescent subatomic particles right around chore time. If they were in motion, a necessary quality for completing chores, you couldn't find them. If you could define their exact position (on the couch in front of the TV), you couldn't get them moving. Looking back, it's amazing how many physics concepts my kids had mastered— including inertia, entropy, and particularly, Heisenberg's uncertainty principle. I owe them a lot.

Okay, let's get back to the idea of energy and matter. Each subtler level of creation contains more energy. At the present gross material level, the energy of the chair you're sitting on supports your weight. At the subtler molecular level of the chair, we will find more available energy. If we rearranged its molecules, say by setting it on fire, we could release a good deal more energy in the form of heat and light. If we want to release even more energy from the chair, we can go to the atomic level. If we knew how to split the atoms of the chair, we could release huge amounts of energy in many forms. I don't know of any work relating to harnessing the power of subatomic particles, but I do know of technologies that utilize subtle wave energy. This is the common abode of the energy healer, and we will explore this very interesting work on our way to learning how to heal without energy.

Each subtler level of creation contains more energy.

Let me ask you this: Have you ever run out of thoughts? I didn't think so. One thing we can say about thoughts is that from our first breath to our last, they are always there. If thoughts are energy and we never run out of them, then it stands to reason that the source of thought is an inexhaustible source of energy. It also stands that we might benefit greatly if we could tap directly into our source of thought.

It turns out that uncovering the source of your thoughts has a definite and overwhelmingly positive healing influence on physical ailments; personal relations; financial success; emotional fitness; and yes, even your love life. Every aspect of your life is wonderfully transformed when you simply become aware of where it all begins. And that would be your ever-present companion, pure awareness.

If thoughts are energy and we never run out of them,
then it stands to reason that the source of thought
is an inexhaustible source of energy.

We just saw that the more refined levels of the material world yield more energy. But where did all that energy come from? By now we know it comes from pure awareness. Creation, by definition, is the movement of energy in some organized or orderly way. Here we need to understand a vital point: Pure awareness is the source of energy without being energy. That means it does not move. It has the potential to create, but it just hasn't done it yet. Neither does it have form. You could say that pure awareness is perfection waiting to express itself.

Pure awareness is the source of energy
without being energy.

Now you may be thinking, *Where is he going with all this?* I'm glad you asked. If you want to play solely in the relative field of life, by all means enjoy yourself. But if you want the greatest power and the most perfect order, you must contact the source of all knowledge: pure awareness. There are thousands of healing modalities that tap into the various levels of life. Bodywork and chiropractic are effective on the gross physical level. Herbs and medications work on the molecular level. Acupuncture and energy healing work with subtle energy waves. But none of these healing forms is designed to draw directly from the source of creation.

This book will teach you the science of healing from awareness. I call this process Quantum Entrainment (QE). Remember, pure awareness is the source of energy and order.

When you perform QE, you are drawing from the purest, most powerful existent available. When you use QE, you will not be doing the healing, awareness will. What's more, you will be healed along with the people you are helping. Talk about your win-win relationship!

CHAPTER 4

THE MIND AND THOUGHTS

"The question is: can you become aware of the reflex character of thought—that it is a reflex. . . . And we could say that as long as the reflexes are free to change then there must be some kind of intelligence or perception, something a bit beyond the reflex, which would be able to see whether it's coherent or not."

— DAVID BOHM

Your mind is a created thing. It is not corporeal like the chair you might be sitting on; it is mental rather than physical. Like matter, it is energy and order. Your mind is the container for your thoughts.

A thought is a very interesting phenomenon. When I was with Maharishi Mahesh Yogi in the early '70s, I spent five months meditating in the sleepy Spanish town of La Antilla. I meditated 10 to 12 hours every day. After the first few weeks, my thoughts became very quiet and I began to see how my mind worked. During that time, I was able to cognize the birth of a thought: each newly created one was a single point of bristling energy at the doorstep of pure awareness. I watched as my own awareness expanded to reveal its contents. Within each thought form was a vibration that represented emotion, logic, and the five senses. Every thought is a galaxy within the universe of mind.

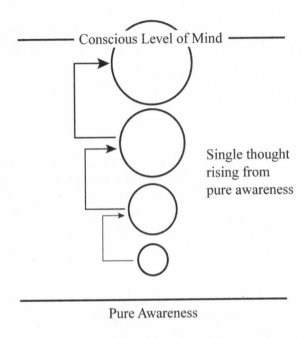

Figure 2: The Mental Model

Once born, the thought would cut its umbilical cord with mother awareness and begin to rise and expand like a bubble rising from the bottom of a pond. The ego is created at the very instant when thought separates from fullness. As it expands, the thought energy becomes dispersed over a greater area. The thought also grows weaker the farther it travels away from its source; it is susceptible to distortion and can become adulterated.

Finally, the thought bursts like a bubble on the surface of the mind. The bursting of the thought bubble, Maharishi later told me, is when the mind becomes conscious of the thought at the end of its journey. It is at that point when we act on our conscious thoughts. I was simultaneously experiencing its birth and death through an expanded awareness resulting from my meditation.

> *Your mind is the container for your thoughts. . . . Every*
> *thought is a galaxy within the universe of mind.*

Each thought has a dominant emotion and sensory vibration. As it expands, the vibrations interact and change. The thought takes its tendency toward action from the dominant inner vibrations. I also saw a kind of matrix through which thoughts would pass on their way to consciousness. If the inner workings had become distorted, this matrix could rearrange the inherent vibrations and change the tendency. Maharishi explained that this was the intellect filtering thoughts, helping to harmonize them so they would become more supportive to one's health and well-being.

There is a lot to be taken away from this experience, but for our purposes, I would like to concentrate on a single point. The farther a thought gets away from pure awareness, the weaker it grows and the more likely it is to be harmful. What we call negative thoughts do not start out that way. They become misshapen by the imbalanced internal pressures of misconception and fear. Once a thought is born, it experiences a kind of separation anxiety.

The Bhagavad Gita puts it this way: "Fear is born of duality." No longer attached to the unbounded oneness of awareness, a thought perceives that it is alone and tries to compensate for its loss. This is when distortion can infiltrate the otherwise perfectly functioning thought. An abhorrent thought is the cause of abhorrent action. We only have to look around us to realize that a purely harmonious, loving, and productive thought rarely finds expression in our day-to-day world.

The farther a thought gets away from pure awareness, the weaker it grows and the more likely it is to be harmful.

If you think I am overly animating the life of a thought, or giving it too much intelligence, don't forget that it is the collection of these very thoughts that have brought you to where you are today. Most people take their basic identity from their thinking. You might say, "I am successful in my job," "I believe in free education," and "I am angry." But what was necessary for you to have success, beliefs, and feelings? Every step of the way, your thoughts have shaped and guided your progress . . . or lack thereof.

The farther a thought has to go to work its way up to our consciousness, the more chances it has to become disharmonious. If we could expand our consciousness in such a way as to contact a thought closer to its origin, then we would diminish the likelihood of disharmony. This is not a new message—in fact, sages have been telling us to get on this bandwagon for eons. The problem is not what to do, but how to do it. Because we have not fully understood the role of awareness in thinking, we have gotten ourselves in a pretty pickle. But it is more than understanding, which takes place in the mind. Pure awareness is beyond the mind, so mere comprehension is out of the question.

Most people take their basic identity from their thinking.

That leaves us with the experience of pure awareness, which is a bit of a sticky wicket as well. To have an experience, we need the mind. And herein lies one of the most salient and almost universally misunderstood tenets for knowing pure awareness: Pure awareness cannot be experienced. We know it by our lack of experience. I only want to mention this here, for no amount of explaining will give us the non-experience of pure awareness. Presently, however, I will show you how to stop your thinking and discover where your own thoughts come from.

> *Pure awareness cannot be experienced.*
> *We know it by our lack of experience.*

CHAPTER 5

THE SPACE BETWEEN YOUR THOUGHTS

"If we could see the miracle of a single flower clearly, our whole life would change."

— BUDDHA

The closer to pure awareness we contact a thought, the more energy and order it has. Contacting a thought at its conception is realizing perfection, free of disharmonious influence.

Before learning Quantum Entrainment, you will be guided through several exercises that will open up your common awareness to *pure* awareness. You only need to tread the path once. It's like wearing a jacket on a chilly day. Once you put it on, it will stay there keeping you toasty warm. Even when you forget you are wearing your jacket, it is still protecting you. At any time you can become aware that you have your jacket on. Likewise, once you have found pure awareness, you only have to become aware of it to know that it is still with you. Are you ready to get started? Okay then, let's go.

Experience 1: Stopping Thoughts

Sit comfortably and close your eyes. Now pay attention to your thoughts. Just follow them wherever they may lead. Simply watch them come and go. After you have watched your thoughts for five to ten seconds, ask yourself the following, and then be very alert to see what happens immediately afterward. Here is the question: *Where will my next thought come from?*

What happened? Was there a short break in your thinking while you waited for the next thought? Did you notice a space, a kind of gap between the question and the next thought? Okay, now reread the instructions, and perform the exercise again. I'll wait. . . .

Did you notice a slight hesitation in your thinking— a pause between thoughts? If you were alert immediately after you asked the question, you will have noticed that your mind was just waiting for something to happen. Eckhart Tolle, the author of *The Power of Now,* says that it is like a cat watching a mouse hole. You were awake, waiting, but there were no thoughts in that gap. You might have heard that it takes many years of arduous practice to clear the mind of thoughts, but you have just done it in a matter of seconds.

Please do this exercise several more times. You can use substitute questions such as *What color will my next thought be?* or *What will my next thought smell like?* or *What will my next thought look like?* The question is not important, but paying attention is. This will expose the gap, the space between your thoughts. *This gap is pure awareness.* It may be fleeting, but it will be there. As you become aware of this mental pause, it will begin to work its magic on you.

Now let's get back to work. Do this exercise for two to three minutes more, reintroducing the question every 15 seconds or so. Pay attention to the gap when it is there, and look for it when it is not. Within just a few minutes, you will notice that your thoughts are calmer and your body is more relaxed.

Why is that? You didn't set out to relax or become peaceful —it just happened naturally, without your trying. Why does becoming aware of awareness make such a big difference in the way one feels and behaves? By being aware, you are able to contact your thoughts at subtler and more refined levels. Each level offers more order and energy. The gap you noticed between thoughts is the experience of non-experience I mentioned earlier. That non-experience is pure awareness.

Flow of Thoughts

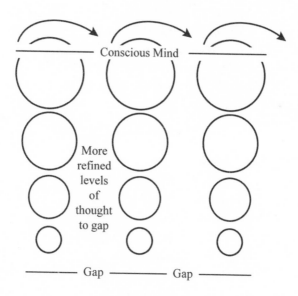

Figure 3: The Gap

Throughout the day, do one-minute meditations where you ask yourself a new question every 15 seconds. You will soon become aware of the space that you found between your thoughts even while you are doing other activities such as talking or driving. If you were to do nothing more than regularly observe this brief interval between thoughts, over time you would notice that you have more energy, less stress, and even a fluid easiness in relationships with others. You might even detect a lighter mood bordering on impishness. Feeling good is fun. This perception is the foundation for more profound and fulfilling experiences to come, but even by itself, this single exercise is worth the price of admission.

Now let's expand our knowledge of the source of thought to draw more deeply from its benefits.

> *The gap you noticed between thoughts*
> *is the experience of non-experience. . . .*
> *That non-experience is pure awareness.*

CHAPTER 6

WHO AM I?

"The only true wisdom is in knowing you know nothing."

— SOCRATES

A few years back Socrates urged us to "Know thyself." Have you ever asked yourself why he felt that was so very important? What possible benefits would befall you if you were to become acquainted with *your* Self? And what the heck is the "Self" anyway? Let's take a look.

Repeat "Experience 1: Stopping Thoughts" from the previous chapter, and rediscover the gap between your thoughts. Do it for several minutes, again asking one of the preparatory questions. Ask a question every 15 seconds or so, remembering to *be very alert to see what happens right after you ask the question.*

Experientially, this gap between thoughts is not much to write home about. It is just a space filled with stillness, obvious only after one thought ends and before the next one begins. Since there is no thinking going on in the interval between thoughts, you won't be aware of it until you start thinking again, and maybe not even then. The mind follows the motion and is enthralled by movement and form, but the gap is free of both. It contains nothing. And nothing means, well, nothing to the mind. But that is a big mistake.

Here is why: all the thoughts in the mind come from that nothing that we have identified as pure awareness.

Test it for yourself. Repeat the exercise and watch the gap. Automatically, and without any effort on your part, the next thought spontaneously arrives. There it is bright as day—a brand-new thought. That's pretty miraculous when you stop to think about it. (Pun intended.) Each new thought is a marvel of creation, and it comes from nothing. So nothing must not be empty. There must be something in there; otherwise, it could not produce a thought. Interesting, isn't it?

> *Since there is no thinking going on in the interval between thoughts, you won't be aware of it until you start thinking again.*

Repeat Experience 1 a couple more times. Above all, remember to be alert and wait to see what happens. By now, you are getting to be an old hand at observing the interval between your thoughts.

Now let me ask you the $64,000 question: *Who is watching the gap?* There are no thoughts, no emotions, no movements of any kind—but you are still there, aren't you? You didn't go into a coma. You didn't go to Tacoma. You were right there waiting for your thoughts to start up again, weren't you? Who was waiting? Who is this "you"? Who is watching when the mind disappears?

When you identify with your thoughts—all balled up in your memories and future plans—you are referring to the "me." *Me* is the collection of *things,* including your age, sex, likes and loves, hopes, and memories that you call your life. But none of that exists the moment your thoughts stop. To observe you must be aware, right? So at that moment when the mind is turned off, you are aware of nothing. There is nothing but pure awareness. Therefore, you have just solved the mystery of who you are. You are awareness!

Who is watching when the mind disappears?

Does that sound impossible? The fact cannot be denied. Your direct perception has revealed your inner Self to be awareness. That's right, before *me* was born and built into the image you recognize as yourself, there was the solitary Self: pure awareness. This is what all the hubbub was about 2,500 years ago when Socrates was asking those probing questions. He made people examine not only the content of their thoughts, but the thoughts themselves. Of course you and I now know that leads very quickly to pure awareness, the indivisible inner Self.

Let's think a little longer on this business about us being pure awareness. Think back on your life and revisit your childhood and adolescence. Now remember times during your 20s, 30s, and so forth until you reach your present age. Think about what you are doing right now. Over your lifetime, your interests and feelings have changed, your body has grown and aged, your family has matured, and your friends have come and gone. But there was a part of you that was with you as far back as you can remember and is still with you today. It has remained unchanged throughout all the phases of your life.

"Me" is the collection of "things," including your age, sex, likes and loves, hopes, and memories that you call your life.

At each stage of your life—no, each second of your life—while your body-mind was busy becoming what it is today, your awareness stood silent vigil, a timeless witness. When you said, "I want my mommy," "I hate gym class," "I will love you forever," or "I don't like loud music," you were identifying things, events, and feelings that were happening to *me* but not to your *Self.* The things and feelings of your life (like wanting your mommy, hating gym class, and so on) all changed and now reside in that part of you called memory. Aspects of your life have changed and continue to do so. But your awareness has remained an unmoving witness to the movie that you call your life.

Alfred, Lord Tennyson spoke to this mystery of enduring changelessness in his poem "The Brook" when he penned: "Men may come and men may go, / But I go on forever." We could just as easily but far less eloquently say that our security, feelings, thoughts, body, and environment may come and go, but our awareness goes on forever. It certainly is not as stirring to the soul, but it does get the point across.

Why is knowing thyself so absolutely vital? When you come to appreciate your inner Self as unchanging, unbounded, eternal awareness, your dependence upon your withering body and failing mind begins to loosen its hold. You become aware that you have surpassed the field of change and even death. You realize that beyond all the things and thoughts that "me" is, you eternally exist as awareness.

You are awareness! . . . Your awareness has remained an unmoving witness to the movie that you call your life.

If just a few minutes of observing the gap between your thoughts brought peace and relaxation, imagine what joyful adventures await you when pure awareness infuses your thinking, eating, working, and loving. Discovering yourself to be pure awareness at the bottom of your mind is the first step to living a full and bounteous life. Teasing awareness into daily activity is the next step. Finally, when you learn to heal your wounds and the wounds of others, it truly is a self-made blessing.

CHAPTER 7

THE GATE TECHNIQUE

"If I had influence with the good fairy who is supposed to preside over the christening of all children I should ask that her gift to each child in the world be a sense of wonder so indestructible that it would last throughout life."

— RACHEL CARSON

I have witnessed all kinds of reactions when people discover that they are pure awareness, and not the stuff and clutter their minds are filled with. Usually there is a moment of delighted surprise accompanied by a sense of freedom and lightness. That sense of euphoria can last for some time, but sooner or later the ego wants to take back control of its mind. When it does, thoughts and things are again elevated to their exalted and exaggerated positions of importance. The frail echo of awareness fades into itself and is quickly forgotten. But this does not have to happen. Hitting all the bases in this book can ensure that you stabilize a mind-set of pure awareness.

The next step to accomplish this is to deepen and broaden the non-experience of pure awareness by increasing the amount of time that you are aware of pure awareness. To achieve this, I have developed a wonderfully simple and ef-fective process that anyone can do. I call it the Gate Tech-nique because it opens the gate to pure awareness as easily as if it had been oiled by the Gatekeeper himself. All you need to do is walk through.

The next step . . . is to deepen and broaden the non-experience of pure awareness.

The Gate Technique creates a subtle yet profound shift in the way you see the world. This *shift* may be barely no-ticeable at first; however, it will deeply influence your body-mind, and from there, all other areas of your life. After just a few weeks of doing the technique, it is not uncommon to have friends comment on your relaxed features or the soft luminescence reflecting in your eyes.

It's time we got started, so roll up your sleeves and get ready to open the gate to your Self.

Experience 2: The Gate Technique

(*Note:* You can download a free MP3 version of the Gate Technique at: **www.QuantumEntrainment.com/down loads.html** or **www.hayhouse.com**. In this audio record-ing, I will lead you step-by-step through the process.)

Sit in a comfortable chair where you will not be disturbed for 10 to 20 minutes. Close your eyes, and let your mind wander for 10 to 20 seconds. Now go through a list of positive words in your mind. You might see the words in your mind's eye or hear them; it doesn't matter. Examples might be: silence, stillness, calmness, peace, joy, bliss, or ecstasy. You may also see or hear other words such as: light, love, compassion, space, infinity, pure energy, existence, or grace. After you have run through your positive words, go back over them again. Gently pick a word that draws your attention. Next, all you have to do is observe the word. Simply pay close attention, and wait to see what it will do.

As you innocently watch, without interfering, your word will eventually change in some way. It may get bigger or brighter or louder. It might start pulsating, or it may get fainter and even fade away and disappear. There is no telling what it will do, but that doesn't matter. Your job is to purely observe, without controlling or interfering in any way. It is like watching TV, but in your mind. How easy can this be?

As you watch your word, your mind might shift to other thoughts, or you may start hearing sounds coming from around you. For a while, you may forget that you are doing the Gate Technique. You could lose yourself in your thoughts, sometimes for minutes at a time. No biggie. If this happens, when you realize that you are not observing your word, just serenely find it again. That's it! The power of the Gate Technique is in its simplicity and innocence.

Now, one last thing, you may notice that your word occasionally disappears. That's okay. Just observe the space it left behind. You will recognize it as the gap where pure awareness abides. The gap is not a goal. It is only another of the many changes your mind will go through. Soon, all by itself, your word will return. Or it may turn into another word. That is okay, too. Just accept the new word, and watch or listen to it as you did the old one.

To review, sit quietly with your eyes closed. After a few seconds, find your word and simply observe what happens.

Don't interfere—just watch. When you realize that other thoughts or noises are present, quietly find your word and begin observing again. If you lose your word, it will return or another one will take its place. Just follow along.

The power of the Gate Technique is in its
simplicity and innocence.

It doesn't matter what happens as long as you purely observe, uninvolved, what is unfolding before you. Continue the Gate Technique for 10 to 20 minutes. (Always get in at least ten minutes if you can.) When finished, do not open your eyes quickly or jump up and start doing things right away. Keep your eyes closed, and take another minute or two to stretch and slowly come back to the outside world. If you come out too quickly, you may feel some irritability, or get a headache or other physical discomfort. Whether you notice it or not, your body will be very relaxed, and it needs time to transition to full activity. Your mind will want to get going, but be sure to give your body a chance to catch up—then slide easily back into your active life.

Do the Gate Technique at least once every day. However, practicing it twice a day quadruples its effects. The best time is as soon as you wake up and then sometime later. If you can't squeeze it in during the day, do it before bed. This will blissfully dissolve the stresses of the day and make for a great night's sleep.

Consistent practice is important for continued success. In the beginning, reread these instructions or listen to the Gate Technique audio download every couple of days. This will erase any bad habits that may inadvertently work their way into the practice. It is common to think you are doing it correctly only to find that you have left something out or added something unnecessary. If you aren't careful to maintain innocent observation, the Gate Technique will not be as effective, and you will find yourself thinking that it is not working as well as it did in the beginning. This is a dead giveaway that some impurity has crept into your practice. After two weeks of checking your technique every couple of days, reread or replay the instructions every two weeks. This will ensure that you benefit fully from your consistent practice.

The Gate Technique teaches you to rely on nothing other than observation. What happens is quite magical. A deep healing begins without a glimmer of effort. Actually, effort of any kind is counterproductive. What the technique effectively does is bathe your psyche in the healing waters of awareness. You are actually aligning with the wisdom that made your body-mind.

When done regularly, you will experience greater energy, physically and psychologically; more relaxation; less illness; more resistance to mental and emotional stress; and improved relationships. All this is accomplished by simply paying attention. Very quickly you will notice that you are observing more and more outside of the Gate Technique during your daily activities. This technique is perfect by itself or can be added to the beginning of other practices to enhance their effectiveness. Just be sure not to change the Gate Technique itself. Remember that its power is in its simplicity; it is complete as it is. Adding to or removing anything will only make it less effective.

A deep healing begins without a glimmer of effort. . . .
All this is accomplished by simply paying attention.

Soon you will be learning Quantum Entrainment (QE), the scientific method of instant healing. While the Gate Technique is not used directly in the QE process, it does help to rarefy awareness, which is the cornerstone of QE. Done daily it will quickly establish the habit of present awareness in activity. Later, when you are proficient in healing, you can substitute QE for the Gate Technique, although many people continue to do both.

Now it is time to examine what Quantum Entrainment is and how it works. Then you will learn how to harness its power so that you can actually heal yourself and others.

CHAPTER 8

QUANTUM ENTRAINMENT (QE)

*"God doesn't look at how much we do,
but with how much love we do it."*

— MOTHER TERESA

What Is Quantum Entrainment?

Quantum Entrainment is a quick and effective scientific method that reduces pain and promotes healing. It creates immediate changes that can be seen and felt in the body. It is reproducible and will stand up to the scientific rigor of pre- and post-testing. QE continues to work long after the initial session, gently balancing and eliminating blocks to physical and emotional well-being. It enlivens a healing awareness in both the initiator and the receiver of the process. There is generally a feeling of peace and relaxation that accompanies a QE session.

Quantum Entrainment wakes you up to your own inner awareness. When you become more familiar with pure awareness, you will feel better in every way. When you become healthier and happier, it's only natural to want to share it with others. Soon you'll learn the QE method of instant healing, and then the cycle will be complete.

You will have learned to give what you get—or more accurately, to share what you are. As it turns out, the people you share your awareness with are also pure awareness. You will simply be awakening them to their basic nature. I would like to expand on that fascinating concept, but it is a journey that would take us well beyond the confines of this book. If you would like to read more about your basic inner nature as it relates to health, relationships, and happiness, I recommend you pick up a copy of my book *Beyond Happiness: How You Can Fulfill Your Deepest Desire*. It makes pretty interesting reading, if I do say so myself. Okay, okay, let's get back on track and leave this shameless self-promotion behind.

> *Quantum Entrainment wakes you up to*
> *your own inner awareness.*

Pure awareness, we will soon discover, is a powerful regenerator of things gone wrong. Symptoms such as pain, confusion, and depression tell us that something is amiss. They serve as signposts that point toward a breakdown within. Whether it is a broken leg or a broken heart, a disorder runs counter to a smoothly functioning, productive, and loving body-mind.

Health is order. The more order we reflect, the healthier we are. When our health begins to break down, we have a multitude of medicines and therapies aimed at reestablishing that order. We can simplify this by looking at it from a vibrational point of view. A vibration, or wave, is the simplest expression of energy. Stars and frogs, angels and anvils, are nothing more than conglomerates of energy waves that coalesce to create those very forms.

We can look at our organs, tissues, thoughts, and emotions as individual bundles of vibrations that work together to create a healthy body-mind. When vibrations get out of sync, we call it a disorder or disease, and then try to heal it. Most healing is accomplished by introducing orderly vibrations to neutralize the disorderly ones. For instance, the herbal vibration of white willow bark will neutralize the inflammation vibration of a headache.

> *Health is order. The more order we reflect,*
> *the healthier we are.*

The process of strengthening or weakening vibrations is called *interference*. I think the simplest way to view it is this: Amplitude is the vertical part of a wave (how high it is). If you add two waves of the same amplitude together, you end up with one big wave that is twice the amplitude of the original. This is called *constructive interference*. The opposite is also true: If you add two waves of exactly the opposite amplitude, they cancel each other out and you end up with zero amplitude. This is called *destructive interference*.

Constructive Interference

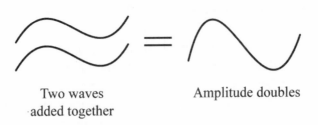

Two waves
added together

Amplitude doubles

Destructive Interference

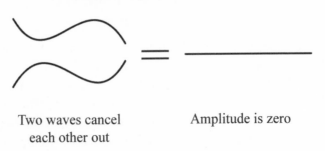

Two waves cancel
each other out

Amplitude is zero

Figure 4: Wave Interference

Don't let all this constructive-destructive interference jargon boggle your inner workings. Go down to the seashore and watch the waves roll in, and you will see this principle at work. As you watch, you will soon see that a faster wave will overtake the slower one in front of it. The two merge and make a single, stronger wave. The momentum of that bigger, faster-moving wave pushes it farther up the beach than the other waves, soaking your brand-new wing-tip tennies. *That* is constructive interference.

As that wave washes back down the beach, leaving your feet submerged to the ankles in a pool of sandy seawater—while you unleash a stream of expletives from behind clenched teeth, and mothers up and down the beach sprint frantically to cover their babies' ears—it meets *another* wave coming in. The force of the outgoing wave reduces the force of the incoming one, which loses size and momentum and falls far short of where you were standing. Not that you would notice, for you are already halfway back to your car, grumbling and sloshing seawater over the tops of your tennies with each step. The loss of momentum by the second wave is an example of destructive interference.

Traditional healing systems such as medicine, acupuncture, bodywork, and subtle energy procedures ultimately work by reestablishing vibrational order. The closer the treatment vibration matches the vibration of the healthy condition, the more complete the healing. Sometimes, a disorder can actually be created by the treatment itself. If the treatment only partially matches the cure, as is the case with prescribed pharmaceutical medications, side effects are created. Generally speaking, the closer the healing system is to working purely with waves or vibrations, the less chance of experiencing side effects. And that brings us back to pure awareness.

Pure awareness is not a vibration, but the source of vibration. It is the potential order and energy behind every form. In theory, if we were somehow able to infuse pure awareness into a disorderly system, perfect order would result without side effects. As it so happens, it *is* possible! That system is called Quantum Entrainment.

Every healing method, system, or procedure is meant to provide direction and support guiding the practitioner over possible hurdles that might prevent him or her from successfully completing the task at hand. We mistakenly think that it is the procedure that is responsible for success . . . but it is not!

Pure awareness is not a vibration,
but the source of vibration. It is the potential
order and energy behind every form.

I am going to let you in on another secret; this one is on the house. It is not the healing procedure, but rather awareness that does the healing. That's right, awareness is the magic ingredient in every successful endeavor. It doesn't matter if you are washing the car, working a trigonometry problem, or clipping your toenails, awareness is always the key ingredient. Just try clipping your toenails without it. Not a pretty picture.

It is not the healing procedure, but rather
awareness that does the healing.

It is your awareness that breathes life into what you do—technique by itself is lifeless. Awareness is like the train, and the procedure is like the tracks: no awareness, no movement. Nothing gets done without awareness. That's why you can pick from any one of thousands of healing forms and still get well.

The Quantum Entrainment procedure puts the emphasis on awareness instead of the procedure. As you will soon experience, the actual technique is almost effortless. In fact, QE really starts working when the procedure stops. That's right, when the structure of the QE technique falls away into pure awareness, healing takes place. You see, the QE procedure is not a healing technique; it is a process to become aware of pure awareness. Healing is actually a side effect of becoming aware. That also means that you are not the healer—pure awareness is. This is an important distinction that will become more apparent as you take up the practice of Quantum Entrainment.

Healing is actually a side effect of becoming aware.

It also brings up a vital point that needs looking at. If you are not the healer, then you cannot take credit for any healing that occurs. You are free from that responsibility, free from that burden.

Let's say that you are asked to help relieve a very painful knee. You do not have to know if the knee is arthritic, sprained, or anything else about it. You do not need to diagnose the problem. The infinite orderliness of awareness will do that for you. You do not need to know anything about the knee. You only need to know what the owner of the knee wants, which, in this case, is to remove the pain.

Once you start the Quantum Entrainment process, the rest is taken care of for you. Actually, not for *you,* but for the person who has the pain. Other than the initial setup, nothing is done by or for you.

Before a QE session, which might last from 15 seconds to several minutes, you will learn how to perform a simple pretest to objectively note the intensity of pain, swelling, and other symptoms. After the session, you will perform the same test and observe to what degree those symptoms have been relieved. Because you were not involved in the healing of the knee, you should not have a vested interest in how the healing has taken place. This saves your ego from bruising and keeps a leash on it. It also allows compassion and the joy of being human to fully blossom. Not bad dividends for a few minutes' work, wouldn't you say?

Quantum Entrainment is simply a process that allows awareness to expand into pure awareness for purposes of healing. Once the initiator of the QE process becomes aware of pure awareness, the actual healing takes place instantly. Although the discordant elements of any illness or condition become integrated in an instant, the results may take some time to fully manifest. Quantum Entrainment will continue to work long after the session is performed. This is another reason why you shouldn't get too wrapped up in the initial results. Let's say that the painful knee was 80 percent improved after the initial QE session. Two minutes later it could be 90 percent improved, and two days after that the pain may be completely gone.

Once the initiator of the QE process becomes aware of pure awareness, the actual healing takes place instantly.

So whatever happens will happen for the best. It is impossible to do harm. The ancient guiding dictum of the healer, "Above all else, do no harm," does not apply to QE for two reasons: you are not healing, and pure awareness can do no harm.

But you are not left out of it altogether. The beauty of the QE experience is that it heals both the partner and the initiator. (Note: We will refer to the person receiving QE as the *partner* and the person who is performing QE as the *initiator*.) By virtue of the process, the initiator easily slips into a sublime state of pure awareness and then allows the perfect harmony of that subtle ground state to re-create or reorganize matter without disorder. When done regularly, this state of inner awareness begins to be felt outwardly, organizing and healing our every thought, word, and action. The experience is peaceful, uplifting, and inspiring.

In the next few paragraphs, I'm going to generally compare and contrast Quantum Entrainment to other healing systems. This is for your understanding. Please don't misunderstand my intentions. I am not commenting about the value of these methods. Every method of healing is precious and necessary. Just ask the millions whose quality of life is improved daily by their use. I am looking at a bigger picture of health, expanding it beyond the body and mind to encompass every realm of human interaction. We are truly limited by the conceptual chains that bind our minds and weaken our bodies.

The beauty of the QE experience is that it heals both the partner and the initiator.

You may only want to use Quantum Entrainment to heal a physical or emotional pain, and that is fine. More than just a method for healing body and mind, however, QE flows easily outward to heal and enrich every human endeavor and beyond. And it all happens automatically. When it is applied regularly, the sharp angles and hard surfaces of life soften. The result is that you come to know life as nurturing—a universal mother who protects, teaches, and ultimately fulfills all your needs. This comes quickly when you rouse from your slumber to greet the new day with a sense of playfulness and awe. QE is the first toy out of the toy box and the last to be returned.

More than just a method for healing body and mind, however, QE flows easily outward to heal and enrich every human endeavor.

When we play with QE daily, our personal ills begin to heal by themselves. Our healing is accelerated. We come to rely less and less on outside modalities and turn more easily inward to become a loving witness of life as it manifests through us. Like a snowball rolling downhill, we gather to us the fullness of life, increasing the momentum of health and vibrant living as we go.

But I am no purist, and I don't think you should be either. Quantum Entrainment has the potential, and I stress the word *potential,* to be the magic bullet for problems of every sort. Each day you will surprise yourself by performing little miracles. This experience will alter the basic foundation upon which you perceive the world. . . . I mean, come on, tapping into the creative source of the entire cosmos?! I dare you to do so and maintain a business-as-usual attitude.

Each day you will surprise yourself
by performing little miracles.

What sets QE apart is that it does not rely on medicines, modalities, and mind-sets. Where a traditional healing system embraces structure, QE looks to dissolve it. The orderly dissolution of structure opens the mind of the practitioner to pure awareness, which in turn adds order to structure.

All methods of healing have value. That value increases as the awareness of the practitioner increases. QE, like every other healing form, is limited by the mind of the practitioner. In a perfect world, Quantum Entrainment would be all we would need to ensure ideal health and harmony in body, mind, relationships, work, spiritual pursuits, education, and recreation. Yes, it can restore harmony in all of these areas. The bad news is that like all healing procedures, QE is limited by the limitations of the practitioner. The good news is that the practice of QE actually removes those limitations. Simply put, the more we practice, the more fun and fulfilling life will be. Now let's turn our attention back to the nuts and bolts of Quantum Entrainment.

The bad news is that like all healing procedures,
QE is limited by the limitations of the practitioner.
The good news is that the practice of QE
actually removes those limitations.

Quantum Entrainment is not a subtle energy procedure. QE does not employ wave interference or in any way try to neutralize abhorrent energy with herbs or medications, bodywork or manipulation, radiating energies, or any other modality. Quantum Entrainment is unique in this respect and here's how.

Any major system of healing, be it traditional medicine, subtle energy, or anywhere in between, requires rigorous study and practice under the guidance of a qualified practitioner to safely and effectively apply it. More than likely, that system evolved over many years of trial and error before it was accepted as viable. Most healing systems are still evolving. They are as much an art as they are a science, and results vary based on the skill of the practitioner. All this caution and attention to detail is necessary because these systems can do harm if not properly applied. Or at the very least, they would be ineffective.

None of this applies to Quantum Entrainment for one simple reason: ultimately, the initiator doesn't do anything. He or she lets pure awareness do all the work. Remember, pure awareness is perfect order. If something appears to be in disorder, pure awareness will fix it. The initiator just sets the stage, getting everything ready and stepping out of the way. Pure awareness then dissolves the disharmony and reassembles it in perfect working order while the initiator looks on in adjunct bliss.

How hard is it to learn Quantum Entrainment? It's as easy as thinking. The practice requires no special skills and can be picked up quickly. In fact, it takes more effort to read about QE than to actually do it. So if you are reading this book, you will be able to learn and apply QE. Then you will experience for yourself the phenomenal curative effects of pure awareness.

What is Quantum Entrainment good for? If you can think it, QE can fix it. It *can* fix it, but that's not to say it *will*, however. Anything that pure awareness made, which just happens to be everything, pure awareness can fix. That makes sense, doesn't it?

Pure awareness is what does the fixing—not the initiator. It is not hampered by our personal needs, aspirations, prejudices, hopes, fears, goals, failures, or anything else bouncing around inside our craniums. We humans see an incredibly tiny sliver of what is, has been, or will be. Our problem is that we think we have a pretty good idea of what is best in any given situation, but the truth is we haven't got a clue. Our world is a sea of cause and effect. Every present cause is the result of infinite and interrelated effects reaching back countless eons to that first gentle thought that spawned the wellspring of creation.

How is it possible to know the primal root that caused the thought you are thinking this very moment? Do you know what made you think that thought, or the one before it?

> *It takes more effort to read about QE than to actually do it. . . . If you can think it, QE can fix it.*

Is it so hard to imagine that we are not the masters of our fate we think we are? Consider a lifelong bachelor who, as a young man, was a minute late leaving for the grocery store because he misplaced his car keys. He arrived at the store a minute late and just missed meeting the only woman he could have ever loved. One minute, one second, can change a lifetime.

We have all speculated at one time or another how our lives would have been different if we had bought one more lottery ticket or had not gone against our parents' wishes and became a street mime. Isn't every moment of our lives filled with forces beyond our control that could completely alter our future?

Let's take a break and play with a little abstraction, okay? Stretching the boundaries of the mind is always good and is especially useful when exploring new healing paradigms. If nothing else, it will give the brain something to chew on. Like a seed, it could sprout and grow into something useful and ultimately quite magnificent.

Quantum physics has exposed several viable theories of multiple universes. One I subscribe to is that every one of us has an infinite number of lives. It is not theory but a mathematical fact that time does not flow. It does not exist as we normally think of it. Our minds create the sequencing that we identify as time. In other words, time is a human creation that does not exist outside our minds. It is only our limited consciousness that confines us to one time and one life.

*Time is a human creation that does not
exist outside our minds.*

It is a strong possibility that you exist in a parallel life just as you are with the exception of one minor change. For instance, in one life you might have arthritis in your fingers; in another, you might have it in your fingers and knees; and in a third, you might have no arthritis at all. Think about it: infinite expressions of you existing side by side. Wouldn't it be amazing if you could consciously move from one to another? Your experience of life would be infinitely expanded, limited only by your consciousness. . . . And now we are coming to a very interesting point.

What connects these multiple universes together? If each of your lives were a pearl on a necklace, what would be the thread that held them together? The unifying thread of multiple universes is Bohm's unbounded whole, the implicate order of pure awareness. Pure awareness is the portal to each of your lives. This may be how Quantum Entrainment works, by moving your consciousness through the portal of pure awareness to a parallel life. If you have arthritis in this life, you effortlessly plunge into pure awareness and come back out free of arthritis in another.

That reminds me of one of the books in C.S. Lewis's The Chronicles of Narnia series, where his characters could dive into a pond and surface in the world of Narnia. It seems that Lewis was intuiting what quantum physics is calling multiple universes.

I like to see it as if it were a music CD. Each track on the surface of the disc would represent a life. The laser light that reads the information sweeps along the CD releasing the music of each life locked within those tracks. The laser is our consciousness sweeping along the track we call our present life. Our consciousness moves from birth to death, but we must remember that there is no motion in time. This is a fact. Time is an illusion created by our conscious mind. All of our lives exist simultaneously just like all the tracks exist at one time on the CD. Now, what if, instead of the laser light moving predictably along one track after another, we could make it skip to a parallel track? We could start playing the parallel track, couldn't we? The instantaneous healing of an entire illness seems like magic until we realize that we just dived into pure awareness from one life and surfaced in another, free of that limiting disease.

I bring this up for a very good reason. The wonders we can perform are limited only by our consciousness. We are all limited, every one of us. It is unavoidable. But knowing what we now know, we can begin to slip through the chains that bind our consciousness and live beyond our present limitations. Could curing our arthritis be as simple as switching tracks on a CD? Yes, if we know how and our minds will allow it. Built within the simple process of Quantum Entrainment are the mechanics of creation, the ability to open our awareness to the infinite possibilities that creation has laid before us.

The wonders we can perform are limited
only by our consciousness.

Now, theory is fun to play around with, and it has the potential to expand your mind beyond its present parameters, but Quantum Entrainment works whether or not you have a theory. It works whether or not you believe in it, and it even works if you don't understand how it works. A child can perform QE with perfect innocence—in fact, it will not be effective without it.

We cannot create this shift in pure healing consciousness through sheer force of will. We can only place our innocent intention in the ocean of pure awareness. Where the currents of harmony and healing lead is beyond our influence. We can have a desire to heal someone, but that desire comes from the limited us, awash in the ever-turbulent ocean of the mind. It may be an altruistic desire born of compassion for a suffering being, but there is no way we can know how the cosmic blueprint will support that desire. We cannot know what infinite, convoluted course of events has led to this apparent disharmony. Nor can we know in what way it will choose to express harmony once again.

When Quantum Entrainment is performed, there is always a change in the condition. It is possible that a single QE session can set in motion forces that will reverberate throughout the universe before that harmony is realized. As an initiator, all we can do is express our desire to make it right. The result, in whatever form it takes, will be a natural and perfect expression of pure awareness. We simply accept what we see with the knowledge that we cannot possibly know what forces are at work or when they will manifest.

A child can perform QE with perfect innocence—
in fact, it will not be effective without it.

I once had a client who asked me to help her with several problems all at once. She had a sinus headache and upper-shoulder muscle spasms as a result of her work. She was also anemic from six weeks of premenopausal complications. I initiated the QE process for several minutes, after which I noted some slight indication that her body had received the organizing influence of pure awareness. When I asked her how she felt, she said that she felt exactly the same as before her session. I explained that the process was successful and that I could do no more for her now. I could see the disappointment on her face as she turned to leave.

About an hour later, however, I got an excited call from my client. She told me that while driving home, the floodgates on her sinuses burst open, and she almost had to stop the car to tend to her now freely flowing sinuses. After she had been in her home for about 20 minutes, her shoulders relaxed and she felt light and unburdened. I congratulated her and thanked her for taking the time to keep me updated on her condition. The next morning she called again, even more excited this time. She was completely free of any premenopausal symptoms.

It is possible that a single QE session can set in motion
forces that will reverberate throughout the universe.

At the time QE was applied, my client had no outward indication that it had worked. I was aware of only the slightest change in a single muscle in her upper back. I didn't know what relief, if any, she would experience. I was saved from all that because I was more like a bystander in the process. I initiated QE and stepped out of the way. I took great joy in the relief of her symptoms, not because I did something, but for another reason. Every time healing occurs in this way, it is testimony that life is vaster than thought and more bounteous than imagination.

When I initiate the QE process, I touch something that is greater than me and I come to know it as my Self. I have a feeling that is not hope, really, but a knowing that everything is right with my world. I don't perform QE just to make my life better. I do it to remind myself that perfection already is, to make ripples on the pond of immortality, and watch as they playfully lap against the lives of my fellow travelers in this infinitesimally small slice of the universe.

CHAPTER 9

PREPARING TO HEAL

*"Think left and think right and think low and think high.
Oh, the thinks you can think up if only you try!"*

— D<small>R</small>. S<small>EUSS</small>

Preparing to apply Quantum Entrainment is not so much a gathering of tools and techniques as it is a preparation to do nothing. Those who know me well are not surprised that I discovered and developed QE. They are quick to point out, in fact, that I have been preparing to do nothing most of my life. It's nice to have such observant and supportive friends.

The first thing I would like is for you to demonstrate to yourself the power of awareness by creating an observable change in your body. By performing this striking exercise, you will not only get the simple basics for healing but you will also get a little taste of the joy and delight of healing Quantum Entrainment style. Ready? Let's get started.

Experience 3: The Growing-Finger Exercise

Hold up your hand, palm facing you, and find the horizontal line, or crease, that runs along the bottom of your hand at the top of your wrist. Locate the same horizontal crease on your other hand, and place your wrists together so that the two creases line up exactly with each other. Now carefully bring your palms and fingers together. Your hands should line up perfectly in prayerlike fashion.

Look at your two middle fingers. They will either be even in length or one will be shorter than the other. For this exercise, you will pick the shorter finger. If your fingers are even, you get to choose either the right or the left one.

Separate your hands and place them in your lap or on a table (if you're sitting before one). Look at the middle finger you chose and think, *This finger will grow longer.* Don't move the finger; just become acutely aware of it. You can do this with your eyes open or closed—it doesn't matter. Look at the finger or envision it in your mind. Focus all your awareness on that single finger; that is all. Do so for one full minute. You don't have to tell it again to grow longer. Once is enough. Just provide what it needs to make the transition, which is *focused awareness.* That one finger gets your total attention for a full minute.

After the minute has passed, measure the length of your fingers using the creases across your wrists exactly as you did before. Note the lengths of your two middle fingers, and presto . . . the finger that received your awareness will be longer! That's pretty amazing when you stop to think about it. (Yes, pun intended.)

⁓

Welcome to the wonderful world of heightened awareness. You've just witnessed how the force of awareness can animate the body and prepare it for healing from within. But how were you able to perform this magical feat (or should I say magical finger)? Let's find out.

The basics for this exercise were intention and awareness. First, you had the single intention for the shorter finger to grow longer. Then you focused all your awareness on that finger. This exercise gets us in the neighborhood of Quantum Entrainment, but you are not quite there yet. You only need to add one additional element, the *Eufeeling,* and you will be ready to become a healing dynamo.

CHAPTER 10

FEELINGS AND EUFEELINGS

*"Happiness is a butterfly, which, when pursued,
is always just beyond your grasp, but which, if you
will sit down quietly, may alight upon you."*

— NATHANIEL HAWTHORNE

What is the difference between anger, pride, worry, sorrow, and other similar feelings and the *Eufeelings* (short for *euphoric feelings*) of peace, joy, and bliss? Simply put, feelings are conditional and Eufeelings are not. Feelings are created by other feelings, thoughts, and circumstances; Eufeelings arise directly out of pure awareness.

When you get angry, you do so for a reason. For instance, you may be angry with your spouse for leaving the cap off the toothpaste tube. You may be sad because someone close to you is no longer in your life. You may be worried because you can't pay your bills. There are conditions for all feelings whether you are aware of them or not.

Eufeelings are unconditional feelings. They do not have or need a reason for being. They just are. For instance, peace exists wherever we are at all times. Once you know how, you can find peace, like the eye of the storm, even in the middle of an emotional hurricane. When you are Self-aware,

aware of pure awareness, you will experience peace along with whatever else you are thinking or doing. You may even recognize that it has been there all along, but you haven't been paying attention to it.

Peace is your natural state of being when you are not caught in the emotional milieu of everyday conditional feelings. If you are unfamiliar with pure awareness, you may find the previous statement hard to believe, but you won't after learning Quantum Entrainment. The QE process naturally and easily brings your everyday awareness to pure awareness and the Eufeelings that shimmer in the subtlest reaches just beyond your mind.

Eufeelings arise directly out of pure awareness.

Conditional feelings are creations of the mind and are caught in time. They serve the needs of the ego to divide and conquer. All conditional feelings have opposites—for example, happiness has sadness and love has hate. And they are always associated with the past or the future. Eufeelings have no opposites. They are ethereal melodies of pure awareness gently lapping against the remote shores of the mind. Always singing but seldom heeded, they are the first and faint articulations of the eternity that we are.

The primal Eufeeling of peace can also be known as silence, stillness, joy, bliss, unconditional love, ecstasy, and the experience of the awe of oneness. Any single Eufeeling contains within it all Eufeelings. In peace is stillness. If you are observant, you will find peace to be joyful. If you are especially quiet, you will find the innocence of unbounded love, too, ready to enfold you in its subtle embrace.

While Eufeelings stand on their own, they can produce conditional feelings in the mind. For instance, when you experience pure joy, it may arouse feelings of pleasure or happiness in your mind. The Eufeeling from the cusp of the mind is perceived as happiness. In this case, the conditional feeling of happiness still needed a reason for being, and that reason was the Eufeeling of joy. Conditional feelings such as anger and lust produce other conditional feelings, but they can never produce Eufeelings.

Once you know how, you can find peace, like the eye of the storm, even in the middle of an emotional hurricane.

This is a very important point to ponder. We must discriminate between feelings generated in the mind to appease the ego's need for dissension and the Eufeelings that support infinite harmony and peace. If we do not, we will remain chained to the whirling wheel of emotional turbulence that has brought the world to the threshold of annihilation. Once understood, it is easy enough to remedy. Experience first the universal harmony of peace, joy, and love; and let the healing unfold spontaneously from within.

If the mind were a lightbulb, then pure awareness would be the electricity that makes it light up. Eufeelings would be the light that is produced by the electricity moving through the filament. Conditional feelings would be alterations in the glass of the bulb, such as color, printing ("60 W," for example), or distortions such as bubbles or wrinkles. To carry the analogy a little further, if you were feeling a bit depressed, your bulb might be blue; if you were angry, your bulb might be red; and so on. Even when the glass of the bulb is blue, the light inside is still pure and clear. It doesn't radiate blueness until it passes through the blue glass of the bulb. Eufeelings are always clear and pure. Even when you are depressed or angry, Eufeelings are still present. But when you identify with your "blueness," you miss the purity of the peace that always resides inside.

If the mind were a lightbulb, then pure awareness
would be the electricity that makes it light up.

Not to stretch this analogy too far, but we can use it to make another important point. When we see people who are depressed, angry, irritable, obnoxious, and so forth, we tend to focus on the "color" that they are radiating. We concentrate on the emotion and miss the purity behind it. When we perform Quantum Entrainment, we become aware of Eufeelings as part of the process. They add momentum to the healing. As we continue with the practice of QE, over time we become more familiar with the primary purity before the thought or action is performed. This knowing quickly spills over into our daily life, and we spontaneously begin to recognize the peace, joy, and unbounded love behind the behavior.

Because we know pure awareness in ourselves and recognize it in others, we are less influenced by another's negative behavior. This leaves us free to enjoy whatever Eufeeling we're experiencing at the time. We not only become more tolerant and loving toward others but we are also gentler with ourselves. Accepting our own apparent imperfections and the behavior they spawn is a wonderful freedom and the foundation for living every day in peace.

CHAPTER 11

QUANTUM ENTRAINMENT AND INTENTION

"He who chooses the beginning of a road chooses the place it leads to."

— HARRY EMERSON FOSDICK

The main ingredient, as it were, of Quantum Entrainment is *pure awareness*. As pure awareness reflects in your mind, it creates the second ingredient: *Eufeeling.* And the final component of QE that we need to discuss is *intention.*

Intention gives direction to pure awareness, providing form to the formless. When you get a meal at a drive-through restaurant, for instance, you place your order at the menu board, make the short drive to the service window to pay, and then pick up your food. What goes on inside the restaurant really doesn't concern you. QE is a lot like ordering a "happy meal." You simply place your healing order, take a little trip through pure awareness, and the results are waiting for you when you arrive at the window of life. Corny, yes, but I think it gets the idea across. Intention is the part where you place your order. How simple can this be?

Intention gives direction to pure awareness.

There are all kinds of intentions in this world. Some are simple and some are quite complex, right down to the tenth decimal place. For our purposes, simple is better, and the QE intention is so simple that it almost doesn't exist. In regard to QE, we say, "The QE intention is implied," meaning that you or your partner already know what needs to be done. Your partner's intention is the reason why he or she is there. (Remember that a "partner" refers to the receiver of QE, which is conducted by the "initiator.")

For instance, if your partner has stomach pain, then the intention is to get rid of that pain. The intention doesn't have to be stated; it is implied by the very presence of that person. It seems that pure awareness, the progenitor of all that exists, knows what needs to be fixed and how to get the job done.

Now get this: initiators don't even have to know what is bothering their partners! That's right—they can keep their problems to themselves, and QE will still work. This is especially valuable when working with emotional discord. Partners can keep their private emotional baggage to themselves. While QE is unpacking their baggage, initiators get to hang out in pure bliss.

One last thing to note is that we are not fighting a battle against pain or anything else. Pain is not an enemy, but an anomaly. Pain is like a misbehaving child who needs love and direction. But we don't have to do anything because the love and direction are supplied by pure awareness.

The QE intention is more like an invitation for pure awareness to be the honored guest of our body-mind homes. And in return, pure awareness loves our misbehaving pains and problems. All disharmony eventually dissolves in the loving embrace of pure awareness.

CHAPTER 12

FINDING PURE AWARENESS

"Awareness is primordial; it is the original state, beginningless, endless, uncaused, unsupported, without parts, without change."

— SRI NISARGADATTA MAHARAJ

Quantum Entrainment is so simple and yet so remarkably effective because it draws on the infinite healing orderliness of pure awareness. It stands to reason that the initiator of the QE process should know what pure awareness is and how to contact it, or more accurately, become aware of it.

The notion of pure awareness has gotten a good deal of press over the years. For the most part, those who have written about it say that it is very hard to attain and takes years of study and practice to get a handle on. I say that it is impossible to attain and you will never get a handle on it . . . *because you already have it.* You can't seek something you already possess. It's not hard—it's impossible.

This is probably why so many of us have had such difficulty realizing pure awareness. We believe it is something that can be figured out, something that can be grasped with the mind. But because pure awareness is essentially nothing, we cannot grasp it with the hand or the mind. We can't even experience it. And this is an important point, too.

> *You can't seek something you already possess.*
> *It's not hard—it's impossible.*

Pure awareness can only be known by the lack of experience. You know, just like when you discovered the gap between your thoughts. It was a lack of experience that you realized only after you started thinking again. Pardon my grammar, but the mind doesn't like *nothing*. It wants to play with ideas or anything else that attracts its attention. That's why it makes finding pure awareness so hard. It has to. The mind can't know *nothing*, so it has to make a philosophy to define it and a complicated technique to find it. Then it revels in conditional feelings, such as self-satisfaction and pride, in an effort to convince itself that it was successful . . . but it is actually doomed to failure.

Pure awareness can't be realized by working at it; it can be realized by not working at it. The trick is to keep the mind busy with something else and then point out that awareness was there all along. Once again, go back to how you did this when you found the gap between thoughts. You're going to do this again, but when you finish, you will be able to recognize pure awareness instantly, whenever you want to.

> *Pure awareness can't be realized by working at it;*
> *it can be realized by not working at it.*

The process we will employ is very effective, but somewhat lengthier than the simple "Stopping Thoughts" exercise you did in Chapter 5. You will need to find a comfortable chair and a place where you won't be interrupted for at least 20 minutes. Do not do this exercise lying down the first few times; the mind is more alert when the body is vertical.

There are several ways you can do the Pure Awareness Technique. The most effective is to get the free MP3 audio download from **www.hayhouse.com** or **www.Quantum Entrainment.com/downloads.html**. Your second choice is to read the following Experience 4 text into a recorder, and then play it back when you are ready to try it.

Another way to go through this process is to have someone else read it to you. However, there should be no communication between you and the other person once he or she begins to read aloud. At the end, silence should be maintained for two or three minutes before opening your eyes. Do not communicate with your reader until you are aware of pure awareness with your eyes open.

Finally, as a last resort, you can reread the instructions a couple of times and do the exercise from memory. This will work well but may take several attempts for you to realize pure awareness spontaneously.

If you have any questions, go to the QE website at: **www .QuantumEntrainment.com**. While you are visiting, drop by the QE Forum where you can interact with other "QEers" and even request a free QE session. One way or another, you will quickly come to know pure awareness. In all likelihood, you will need no more help than what you find between the covers of this book, but if you would like more guidance, QEers are always ready and willing to help. Now, let's get to the business of finding pure awareness.

Experience 4: The Pure Awareness Technique

Sit comfortably in your chair with your hands separated. Close your eyes and become aware of your right hand. Do not move it; just be aware of it. Pay close attention to what you feel. Can you feel your pulse or any muscle tension? Do you feel any discomfort or pain? Can you become aware of a generalized sensation, such as hot or cold, relaxation or tingling? (Do this for 30 seconds.)

Now become aware of your left hand in the same way (15 seconds). Then become aware of both hands at the same time (10 seconds). Become simultaneously aware of both wrists (2 to 3 seconds).

Spend 2 to 3 seconds for each body part from here:

- *Both lower arms.*

- *Your elbows.*

- *Your upper arms.*

- *Your shoulders.*

- *Become simultaneously aware of your arms, from your fingertips to your shoulders.*

- *Become aware of the area across your upper back.*

- *Now your middle and lower back.*

- *Your whole back.*

- *Your sides, from your armpits to your hips.*

- *Become aware of your chest.*

- *Your abdominal area.*

- *Your pelvis; then become aware of your whole pelvic region.*

- *Your hips.*

- *Your upper legs.*

- *Your knees.*

- *Your lower legs.*

- *Your ankles.*

- *Become aware of your heels.*

- *Your soles.*

- *The tops of your feet.*

- *Your toes.*

- *Become simultaneously aware of your big toes.*

- *Your second toes.*

- *Your third toes.*

- *Your fourth toes.*

- *Your little toes.*

- *Become aware of your legs, arms, and torso.*

- *Now become aware of your neck.*

- *Your chin.*

- *Your jaw.*

- *Your right ear.*

- *Your left ear.*

- *Your lower lip.*

- *Your upper lip.*

- *Become aware of the line between your lips.*

- *Become aware of your right nostril.*

- *Your left nostril.*

- *The tip of your nose.*

- *Your whole nose.*

- *Become aware of your right eyelid.*

- *Your left eyelid.*

- *Your right eye.*

- *Your left eye.*

- *Your right eyebrow.*

- *Your left eyebrow.*

- *Become aware of the space between your eyebrows.*

- *Your forehead.*

- *The back of your head.*

- *The top of your head.*

- *Your whole head.*

- *Become aware of your whole body. Have awareness of your whole body (10 seconds).*

- *Now become aware of an area around your body—an area about 12 inches around your body, like an oval or egg surrounding your body (10 seconds).*

- *Let your awareness expand further away from your body (5 to 6 seconds).*

From here, hold each object in your mind for 5 or 6 seconds:

- *Become aware of your awareness filling the whole room.*

- *Now expand beyond the room and become aware of your awareness in the whole building.*

- *Expanding beyond the building, become aware of an area around it.*

- *Expanding ever-more rapidly, become aware of the whole city.*

- *Expanding still more rapidly, become aware of the area around your city, neighboring cities, and the whole state.*

- *Become aware of neighboring states and the entire country.*

- *Become aware of all of North America and then of the whole Western hemisphere (or whichever continent and hemisphere you are in).*

- *Become aware of the entire Earth. Become aware of the planet spinning silently, powerfully, on its axis.*

- *Your awareness continuing to expand, the Earth grows smaller, the moon a silver dot.*

- *Earth grows smaller and smaller until it is just a glistening light the size of a star in the sky.*

- *Your awareness continues to expand and the sun slips silently by. It becomes smaller and smaller until it is the size of the other stars in the sky.*

- *You become aware of the millions and billions and trillions of other stars filling the sky. All are within your awareness.*

- *Your awareness continues to expand as the stars form into the galaxy, spiraling silently, powerfully, on its axis.*

- *And still your awareness continues to expand and the galaxy gets smaller and smaller until it is the size of a star in the sky.*

- *It is lost among the millions and billions and trillions of other galaxies in the sky.*

- *As your awareness expands, all the galaxies, all of creation, take the form of an oval or egg suspended and supported by your awareness.*

- *All of creation is contained in this single glistening cosmic egg within your awareness.*

- *As your awareness continues to expand, the egg of creation grows smaller and smaller.*

- *It is the size of a grapefruit.*

- *The size of an orange.*

- *The size of a lemon.*

- *The size of a pea.*

- *The size of a single glistening star in the sky.*

- *As your awareness expands, all of creation becomes the size of a brilliant pinhole of light suspended in your unbounded awareness.*

- *Then all of creation, that single pinhole of light, goes out (30 seconds).*

- *Now once again become aware of your whole body (15 seconds).*

- *Become aware that you are sitting in this room filled with your awareness. Everything in the room is in your awareness (15 seconds).*

- *Become aware that all of creation is in your awareness (15 seconds).*

- *Become aware of your whole body again, sitting in your awareness.*

- *Now take 2 to 3 minutes to remain seated and relaxed before you open your eyes. Maintain your expanded awareness as you begin to open your eyes. Don't be in a hurry. Take time to come out, as your awareness fills the whole room (1 minute).*

- *With your eyes still closed, slowly wiggle your fingers and toes, or stretch lightly. Be aware of your awareness permeating your body and filling the room (30 seconds).*

- *Now slowly open your eyes while you are aware that your awareness fills the whole room (10 to 15 seconds).*

- *Are you still aware of your awareness filling the whole room? Look at any object. Are you aware of your awareness between you and the object? Your awareness has always been there. You are just becoming aware of it outside of yourself. How do you feel (5 to 7 seconds)?*

- *Do you feel some sense of peace or quietness? Some lightness or bliss (5 to 7 seconds)?*

- *The quiet easiness you feel is a Eufeeling. It is a reflection in your mind of pure awareness. It doesn't matter if you feel it as joy, peace, or stillness; it is the result of being aware of pure awareness.*

- *Are you aware of your awareness filling the room right now (3 to 5 seconds)?*

- *See, it is still there. It is always there, and now you will always be aware of it whenever you want. Do it again. Become aware of your awareness in the whole room (3 to 5 seconds).*

- *Now become aware of your awareness in your whole body (3 to 5 seconds). It's there, too! Pure awareness is everywhere. It's like the coat that you forget you are wearing. All you have to do is think about it, and you will know that it is there, always keeping you warm.*

Whenever you think about pure awareness—that is, become aware of it—you will find it waiting for you. Wherever you are, there it is. It's like the young child of a loving mother. When the child misses her mother, she only has to look around to see that her mom is there, watching over her.

- *Go ahead, is "mother" watching? Become aware of your awareness filling the whole room, your body, and all of creation (5 to 7 seconds).*

That took no effort at all, did it? You didn't have to do something to find awareness, did you? You just became aware that it is there. Now you don't need a technique to find pure awareness only to lose it again when you stop the technique. You will be aware of pure awareness forever and without effort. How cool is that!

Okay, one more thing:

- *Close your eyes again and become aware of your awareness filling the room (15 seconds).*

- *Now pay attention to what you are feeling—your Eufeeling. Just identify if you are feeling peace, stillness, quiet, bliss, and so on. Find your Eufeeling, and watch it for a while (8 to 10 seconds). Nice, isn't it?*

- *Now open your eyes. Become aware of awareness all around you, and again identify your Eufeeling with your eyes open. It could be the same or different; it doesn't matter. Just pay attention to what Eufeeling you are having right now (8 to 10 seconds).*

∼

In preparation for creating a healing event with Quantum Entrainment, every now and again throughout your day, I would like you to become aware of pure awareness and the Eufeeling associated with it. For the first few times, you may need to start out in a quiet environment with your eyes closed. But after a couple of tries, you will be aware of your Eufeelings even in the middle of rush-hour traffic.

Remember to become aware of pure awareness first. Then while you are watching, or feeling pure awareness, your Eufeeling will effortlessly shine through. While becoming aware of awareness is effortless, it takes time to get used to a good feeling that is not associated with some activity. The Eufeeling is the subtlest activity in the brain, and it takes practice to get your otherwise active mind used to hanging out on that quiet level.

Okay, that does it for now. I'm glad to have had you along for the ride. Now that you are among the newly awakened, fully savor your new awareness and the joy it will visit upon you.

CHAPTER 13

HOW TO HEAL IN THREE STEPS

*"There are only two ways to live your life.
One is as though nothing is a miracle. The other
is as though everything is a miracle."*

— ALBERT EINSTEIN

Healing with Quantum Entrainment is actually realizing that you are not healing. You are not creating positive energy to overcome negative energy. You are not calling on other forces or formulas to do your bidding. You *are* creating an atmosphere in which healing will take place. QE is tapping into the field (for lack of a better word) of perfect order. From there you do nothing, and everything gets done for you.

As a matter of convention, I will say "You heal" or "I healed," but that is not strictly true. In preparation for creating a healing event, we must adopt the correct angle of entry to be successful. For me to say that we do not perform the healing is neither attitude nor philosophy. It is a simple fact based on observation. This healing presence is not a foreign force that is beyond you but your very own essence—pure awareness reflected through Eufeeling. Nothing more, nothing less.

QE is tapping into the field of perfect order.

You will be amazed by the power your awareness holds, but know that you do not own that power. You are that power and will soon experience it firsthand. You will slip beyond the boundaries that you have meticulously built these past decades in order to define the little you. These boundaries have confined your awareness to thoughts and things that have all served to strengthen your concept of *me*. However, that will be set aside the very first time you experience Quantum Entrainment.

You will be amazed by the power your awareness holds, but know that you do not own that power. You are that power.

Now let's roll up our sleeves and get ready to create a healing event. We'll start with a simple case: a friend has asked you to help him with left shoulder pain and muscle tension in the upper back and neck. With QE, it is not necessary to know the cause of the condition. Healing will take place on the causal level automatically. As the initiator, you only need to know what is desired. Obviously, your partner desires relief from his shoulder pain and muscle tension. That is inferred and is also your intention. It is all the info you need.

Getting Ready to Heal

Before you start, have your partner move his shoulder so that it creates the pain he wants to eliminate. Have him show you how his range of motion is diminished and anything else that demonstrates how the body is affected by this condition. Then ask him to grade the severity of his pain on a scale from one to ten (ten being *unbearable*), and note that number. It's also important to get into the habit of pretesting and posttesting. This will give you valuable feedback, especially in the beginning when you are getting used to the QE process. If you are a physician, use the same tests you would employ for traditional treatment. For instance, a chiropractor might use orthopedic and neurological tests, palpation, and even x-rays to objectively identify the problem and determine the level of improvement.

> *Get into the habit of pretesting and posttesting.*

You only need to be aware of the intention one time. Pure awareness is neither deaf nor dumb. It will know what you want better than you will. Pure awareness will know what to do and when to do it—of this you can be sure. Now you are ready to start.

Triangulation: The Three-Step QE Process

On your partner's shoulder, upper back, or neck, it should be easy to find a muscle that is tight or painful to the touch. Place the tip of your index finger (Contact A) on a tight muscle. Push in firmly so that you can feel how hard or tense the muscle is. Then relax and let your finger rest lightly on the tight muscle. Now lightly place the index finger of your other hand (Contact B) on any other muscle. It does not have to be taut or sore to the touch. Just pick a muscle at random, and place your finger there.

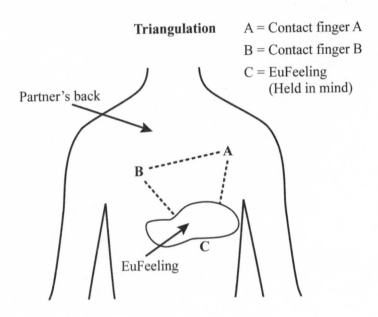

Triangulation

A = Contact finger A
B = Contact finger B
C = EuFeeling
    (Held in mind)

Partner's back

B

A

C

EuFeeling

Figure 5: Triangulation

Step 1: Focus all of your attention on Contact A and become very aware of what you feel. Take the time to notice the heat from the muscle on the tip of your finger, the texture of your partner's skin or clothing, the tightness of the muscle pushing back against your finger, and so on. Become aware of everything you can where finger and muscle meet.

Step 2: Become acutely aware of Contact B, just as you did with Contact A. Then become clearly aware of what both fingers are feeling *at the same time.* Maintain this awareness for several seconds. While you simultaneously hold your attention on both fingers, you will also notice a separate part of you that is watching the whole process take place. You, your awareness, is aware of both fingers. So far, you have awareness of Contact A, awareness of Contact B, and awareness that you are aware of both at the same time. It doesn't matter if you are clearly aware of this phenomenon or not; it is happening naturally, without effort.

Step 3: As you hold awareness of the two points in this expanded way, do nothing. That's right—just pay attention to what you are sensing in the tips of your two fingers and that is all. If you are simultaneously paying attention to your two contact fingers and doing nothing else, you will soon begin to feel a sense of quietness, stillness, or even peace. This is a Eufeeling generated from your expanded awareness. At this point, become aware of this sensation as you hold your awareness on Contacts A and B.

You now have three points of awareness: Contact A, Contact B, and your Eufeeling. Holding them in your awareness is called *triangulation.* Continue to be aware of all three points until you feel a change in your partner's body, particularly in his muscles. (This can take several minutes when you are first learning QE.) The change you experience might be a softening or loosening of the muscles under your fingers. It may feel as if your fingers are relaxing or dissolving into the muscles themselves. Or you may feel that your partner is generally relaxing. His shoulders might loosen, or he may sigh or take a deeper breath. If you are both standing, you might note that your partner is swaying. This is a common reaction to the very deep level of healing rest that your partner is enjoying. You may also notice that your partner is generating more body heat or even sweating.

All of these changes signify that your partner's body is healing. It is reorganizing to eliminate the disorderly pain and tension. After you observe any of these indicators, continue to triangulate by simultaneously being aware of the two contact points and your Eufeeling a little while longer. Then remove your fingers.

Congratulations! You have just completed your first Quantum Entrainment session. With just two fingers and your Eufeeling, you have eliminated your partner's suffering!

You might be wondering what your partner is experiencing while you are creating this healing event. The answer is: Absolutely nothing. Before a QE session begins, I tell my partner: "Just let your mind wander wherever it wants to go." I am often asked by partners if they should relax, meditate, or repeat their own intention. They should do *nothing*. They should not try to help in any way because if they do, it would only slow down or counteract the initiator's efforts. The reason for this is since their minds are busy with other chores, they are less open to the healing influence that QE generates. However, a mind in "neutral" will naturally and effortlessly drop into the healing waters of pure awareness.

Always make your partners comfortable. If they wish, they can close their eyes, but that is all the preparation they need. If they want to help you in some way, you can tell them that the best thing they can do is to allow their mind to wander with no direction or intent.

Quantum Entrainment works very well under the most trying circumstances. Your partner may be in a great deal of physical or emotional pain. You may find yourself performing QE in an emergency room, a crowded mall, or in any other unsettling environment; and healing will still take place. So don't think that you are limited by these things. But given the choice, a serene environment with a compliant partner is always preferable.

The QE Session in a Nutshell

- Partner describes pain (intention implied).

- Pretest.

- Become aware of Contact A (hard or painful muscle).

- Become aware of Contact B.

- Become aware of both A and B at the same time.

- Wait for Eufeeling.

- Hold awareness of A, B, and Eufeeling.

- Observe partner's muscles loosening, body swaying, breathing changes, or other signs of relaxation.

- Posttest.

CHAPTER 14

WHAT TO DO AFTER A QUANTUM ENTRAINMENT SESSION

"This was love at first sight, love everlasting: a feeling unknown, unhoped for, unexpected—in so far as it could be a matter of conscious awareness; it took entire possession of him, and he understood, with joyous amazement, that this was for life."

— Thomas Mann

When you finished your QE session, did you feel relaxed and peaceful? Quantum Entrainment heals the healer as well as the one requesting healing. Both you and your partner should be feeling quieter and more serene. Relaxation is the body's reaction to the healing presence of pure awareness, and peace is the reflection of pure awareness in the mind.

Remember to ensure that your partner is comfortable. The QE experience can be a little disorienting for some people. The sudden rush of pure awareness may take them away from this world for a bit. Afterward, they might need time for their mind and body to reorient to the here-and-now.

If this happens, it generally only lasts a few minutes. Give your partners space until they are ready to resume.

One thing you can count on is that after the QE session, your partner will continue to heal for the next day or two. If you perform a second posttest 20 to 30 minutes after the initial session, you will almost always find that your partner's pain level is getting even smaller as the problem continues to heal. Making sure that your partner transitions easily from the QE session to his or her more active lifestyle will encourage the healing process to continue unobstructed.

*Quantum Entrainment heals the healer
as well as the one requesting healing.*

On occasion, especially after an extended QE session, your partners may need more time to adjust to their new body and may become tired or so relaxed that they don't want to move. If at all possible under these circumstances, make sure your partners get the needed rest. This just means that great amounts of physical and emotional stresses are being released, and a brief repose is the most expedient way for this transition to take place. After all, rest is the universal healer, and pure awareness is the deepest rest possible. If your partners can't lie down and relax right then, suggest that they go to bed early that evening. Then they will awaken to a bright new world and have an extra bounce in their step.

*Rest is the universal healer, and pure
awareness is the deepest rest possible.*

The best time to do your posttest is as soon as you have finished the QE session and your partner is stable. Ask your partner to once again grade his or her condition or level of discomfort on a scale from one to ten. For the example case mentioned in the previous chapter, you would have your partner put his shoulder through the same range of motion, and ask him to grade the pain and muscle tightness as he did before. This is necessary feedback for you in the early stages of learning QE, and it is also good for your partner to get a more objective view of the healing that took place in his or her body.

QE heals so quickly and easily that it often appears as if nothing has happened. The posttest, therefore, is a real eye-opener for many partners. I never get tired of watching people's faces as they perform the posttest, and a pain or restriction they've endured for 30 years is gone in 30 seconds.

QE heals so quickly and easily that it often appears as if nothing has happened.

QE works every time, but not always in the ways you want it to. That is because pure awareness views the big picture and knows exactly how healing should take place. There is almost always a significant relief of symptoms immediately after a QE session, and if the problem is not completely eliminated initially, then it will take just a little more time for the body to adjust. The healing will continue to take place over the next day or so and can even be felt weeks later.

It is not uncommon for me to do QE on a workshop participant in the morning and only see a minor drop on the posttest scale, but by the midday break, the pain is then completely gone. Even though the actual healing takes place instantly (via pure awareness during triangulation), a person's body may require additional time to integrate those corrections physiologically. We'll spend more time on this later.

There is no rule saying that you can't turn right around and do QE again for the same condition. If you think it will help, repeat the session. Or better yet, do multiple applications during a single session. Just keep your A contact and move your B finger to different areas. Or you can move both fingers if you wish, depending on what feels best to do in the moment.

Perform QE as many times as you like. You can do no harm. But let me caution you against thinking that more is better—it isn't. You should have in your mind that one short session will take care of the problem and go from there. In an upcoming chapter, I will show you how to do "Extended QE," but for now, let's keep it very simple. Deal? Good.

For all intents and purposes, you are done. But in the beginning while you are sharpening your QE skills, it doesn't hurt for you to ask your partner a few questions. Find out how he felt during the session or if any other pains are gone along with the original complaint. Inquire after his emotional well-being. Actually, ask any questions you need to know to help you more fully understand the power and potential of QE.

Perform QE as many times as you like.
You can do no harm.

The whole QE process should be delightful. If you find yourself getting tangled up in the instruction, that is natural at first. The steps are seamless, but reading about them takes considerably more effort than actually doing them. Just relax into it and follow the instructions with a sense of adventure and play. Everyone can do QE. You are no different. While this technique is simple and immediately effective, it is a new skill and you will need to practice it often in the beginning. Remember, well begun is half done. The more feedback you gather at this stage, the more quickly you will become proficient at applying Quantum Entrainment.

Practice it on everyone: your friends, family members, neighbors, and even your pets. Soon you will also learn

"Remote QE," which means that you don't even have to have your partner present. You can sit comfortably at home and create a healing event with your friends and family scattered all over the world.

The first several times you practice QE, I suggest that you and your partner both stand. The main reason for doing so is that you will get more precise feedback from your partner. In particular, you will notice her swaying, a sign that pure awareness is working. You will also more easily observe whether she takes a sudden deep breath, which is another indicator that QE is working its magic. It is not as easy to observe these indicators when your partner is seated or lying down.

I would also recommend that you stand a bit behind your partners in the beginning, or at least where they cannot see you. Being out of the line of sight allows them to relax rather than watch you. It doesn't matter for the sake of their healing. Quantum Entrainment will work regardless of your partner's state of mind. It is more for your comfort and concentration, as some initiators are self-conscious when they first get started and can be distracted if their partners are watching their every move.

> *Quantum Entrainment will work regardless of your partner's state of mind.*

Another practical point is that you do not have to put your fingers on the area of complaint. You can touch anywhere on the body and heal any other area, including internal organs.

I was at a book fair promoting my book *Beyond Happiness* when a fellow author approached me. He said that he'd heard I did kind of a weird thing that got rid of pain. I asked what was bothering him. We had been standing for some time, and his arthritic knee had become inflamed and swollen. I pretested him simply by asking him to stand on the knee in a way that increased the pain. Then I had him sit on a box of books. I didn't want to bend way over to place my hands on his knee, so I positioned my fingers on his shoulders. He immediately turned around and reminded me that it was his knee that was hurting. I assured him I was working on his knee.

I formed the intention and began triangulation on his upper-shoulder muscles. Less than a minute later, I asked him to stand as he did before to test the knee. He did and—I never get tired of this part—his eyes opened wide as a sense of wonder lit up his face. Pain free, he returned to his stall to sell more books than I did. My fingers contacted his shoulders, but the intention made sure it was his knee that received the healing.

Sometimes pain (or other symptoms) will worsen before it gets better. Just assure your partner that this is normal. During this time, the body needs to exacerbate the condition for a short period in order for it to heal. Continue to triangulate, and the pain will subside quickly. On rare occasions, your partner might become too uncomfortable to continue. At that point, discontinue the QE session. Perhaps you might perform QE on another problem or just sit quietly. After a few minutes, perform the posttest and see if the condition still exists. If so, do QE again. In all likelihood, the pain will dissolve with no further issues.

One last thing: since you are not doing any healing, you cannot take any credit for the results. This is a very important point. If you do not take credit for the results, you cannot be *attached* to the results. Do you see where I'm going with this? If you are not attached to the results of your QE session, then you are able to accept whatever results appear. Complete acceptance of the fruits of your QE labor, whether more or less than you expected, alleviates mental discord. A mind free of discord is capable of reflecting Eufeelings. And Eufeelings, as you now know, are necessary for healing to unfold.

If you are not attached to the results of your QE session, then you are able to accept whatever results appear.

When you have a healing agenda, you diminish your ability to create a healing event. For instance, let's say the local TV station wanted to do a news brief on your ability to heal based on several remarkable success stories. When they show up, the reporter asks you to perform QE on her indigestion. Feeling that you had better perform admirably or this will be a very short interview, you develop a pretty acute case of performance anxiety.

Not wanting to be embarrassed, you take your A and B contacts and wait for your Eufeeling. You are preoccupied with trying to remove her discomfort and are already thinking about what you will look like on the 6 o'clock news. Your Eufeeling couldn't blast its way into your consciousness with a cannon because you are trying to heal with your thoughts. When the Eufeeling is a no-show, you begin pushing energy and repeating your intention as if you were beating a drum. At this point, you might as well get her a Tums because your dyspeptic mind cannot offer her relief.

It is far easier to start a QE session by letting your partner know that you cannot discern how much healing will result. You might say, "We will accept whatever we get." You should also mention that not everything will be immediately obvious, and healing may continue for several days after the session. Finally, you may want to add that improved results sometimes require additional QE sessions.

Now that you know how to create a healing event, I thought it would be prudent for me to give you some additional ideas that will help you broaden and deepen your healing experience. For instance, I have barely touched on psychological healing, yet this is an area in which QE really shines.

But before we start, maybe I should take this opportunity to state the obvious: Quantum Entrainment can be used for any kind of healing and should always be performed in conjunction with, not instead of, qualified medical treatment. QE is a powerful adjunct to traditional health-care practices. It can only enhance the efforts of other healing systems, increasing the depth of healing and considerably shortening total healing time. Often, if QE is done before seeing the appropriate health-care practitioner, the symptoms will disappear. Even if symptoms abate, one should always consult professional help to be certain that there are no underlying etiologies or additional undiscovered problems.

QE is a powerful adjunct to traditional
health-care practices.

The more you practice QE, the more healing will take place in your own life. Your growing familiarity with pure awareness will spill over into your everyday life, bringing a level of fulfillment undreamed of. Equipped with nothing more than your own awareness, no matter where you go, you can initiate a healing event.

In essence, you are learning to love. Actually, you can't learn to love—you are love. Eternal joy and unbounded love cannot be created. They are already there; otherwise, they wouldn't be eternal and unbounded. They are waiting to be discovered. Pure awareness is pure love. Being aware is un-conditional love in motion. Everyone has heard that love conquers all. Now you have the opportunity to prove it.

As you continue to initiate Quantum Entrainment, you will luxuriate in the joy of helping others and receive their gratitude for sharing this simple, life-changing process. And you are just scratching the surface! Wait till you see what is to come.

CHAPTER 15

PSYCHOLOGICAL HEALING

"You must have failed deeply on some level or experienced some deep loss or pain to be drawn to the spiritual dimension. . Or perhaps your very success became empty and meaningless and so turned out to be failure."

— ECKHART TOLLE

We have been focusing on applying Quantum Entrainment to physical conditions. As remarkable as that is, there's more. "Emotional QE" is a powerful tool for quieting psychological pain. Like physical disharmony, psychological discordance can be removed instantly. It may have its roots deeply embedded in what our mind perceives as the past. Quantum Entrainment does not recognize the past, or even the future. Both concepts are illusions and bind the mind to the ever-deepening spiral of entropy. In other words, the flow of time is created in the mind. This fixation on what was and what will be plants the seed for psychological disease, which can only germinate and flourish under the watchful eye of Father Time.

According to quantum physics, time does not flow. The arrow of time points in the direction of decay. The arrow points but does not move, much like a compass needle points north but does not move in that direction. It is the sweep of our consciousness that creates the illusion of time.

"Emotional QE" is a powerful tool for
quieting psychological pain.

Here's an example: I love to go to the movies. For a couple of hours, I become completely engrossed in the obvious illusion unfolding on the screen. When I step into the theater, I leave my everyday life behind. Although the movie is only a flickering of light and shadow, it represents the greater illusion we call *real life,* which is waiting for us just outside the theater doors.

The illusion of movement is created in our minds when thought oscillates between past and future. Thoughts of future and past construct a mental bridge crossing over the ever-present now of pure awareness. Our consciousness flits from thought to thought missing the pure awareness in between. It is like watching a movie. Movie film is a long strip of individual pictures or frames. In a single second, 24 still frames flash on the screen. This is faster than our brains can individually process, so it looks like the still pictures are in motion, which is pretty amazing. We see motion where there is none. That is the illusion a movie produces.

Our consciousness flits from thought to thought
missing the pure awareness in between.

Likewise, time is the illusion that the mind produces. Individual thoughts are like the individual frames of movie film. Remember that individual thoughts break away from pure awareness and travel to the "screen" of consciousness. They occur so quickly they appear to be moving just like the individual frames of a movie. That illusion of motion is what we call time.

When we think about future events, we are moving forward in time. When we visit our memories, we are moving back in time. All this movement takes place in the mind. It exists nowhere else in the universe. Even though it appears otherwise, our time, our future, and our past are not shared by anyone else.

The movie projector works on a simple principle. A bright white light shines through the film and creates a picture on the screen in the front of the theater. The movement of the film, frame by frame through the light, creates the illusion of movement on the screen. As the audience, we sit contentedly watching the drama of the actors unfold, forgetting that they are merely light and shadow created by a bright light shining through film at the back of the theater. We cry and laugh as if the illusion were real.

Our life is just like a movie. It unfolds thought by thought, minute by minute, year by year. We, the audience, get completely absorbed in the drama of our own movie. We worry over bills, love our new house, watch our children grow up, and contemplate our own death. Like a movie, our lives are an illusion, a play of light and shadow. Don't get me wrong—our lives exist, but not in the way we think they do. This mistaken identity causes an overwhelming suffering that only deepens with each generation.

Emotional QE stops the mind in its tracks and makes it pay attention to right now, robbing it of its preoccupation with the past and future, as well as of its guilt, anger, anxiety, and fear. When we triangulate psychological discord, we shine the bright light of pure awareness on it. This instantly takes us out of movie mode, momentarily off the screen and into the audience. There we can observe the disharmonious emotions and events with healing calmness and clarity. The movie of our life continues to unfold as before but without the influence of those hurtful, afflictive emotions.

How Emotional QE Works

Removing psychological pain is as easy as removing physical pain—perhaps easier. You don't have to know what is causing the emotional distress in your partners. In fact, I strongly recommend that you allow partners to keep their emotional concerns private. This practice is important in two ways. First, it affords your partners a level of privacy that may be welcome, especially if they don't know you well or if they just want to keep their inner life private. Second, you are saved from having to deal with someone else's emotions, which can be draining on your own emotions. And at the very least, it will save you time.

Emotional QE is completely safe. It is not a therapy of any kind. It does not require analysis or training because the initiator does not do anything. QE is accomplished by the partners bathing their emotional discord in the healing waters of pure awareness. The initiator just gets the process started—that's it. You do not have to muck around in a roiling sea of raw emotions. Leave that to the professionals.

*Removing psychological pain is as easy as
removing physical pain—perhaps easier.*

Speaking of professionals, if you are a trained psychiatrist, psychologist, or psychotherapist, you can use Emotional QE with great effectiveness in your practice. You might consider doing Emotional QE right after your first pretesting. Many initial sources of distress could be eliminated with little effort, and you can then focus on what is left with more traditional techniques. Emotional QE will also work wonders for established patients. It can sometimes help break through long-standing blocks and will accelerate the healing process in general.

I once had a partner who was a psychologist with 25 years of experience, and I was able to initiate a life-altering change in her in just a few minutes. She had been lugging around a traumatic experience since childhood. And although she had approached its resolution from many different directions with quite a number of therapists throughout her professional career, she was unable to overcome it. Those few minutes of Emotional QE took place more than six years ago, and she is still emotionally free from this problem. It will not return.

The healing that takes place through Emotional QE is permanent. Fear is the basal emotion from which all others are spawned. Fear, as you may recall, is created when the ego appears to split from pure awareness and takes on its individual identity. It does not matter if your partner is experiencing anger, anxiety, guilt, or sadness; at the bottom of it all is the fear of separation from pure awareness. Emotional QE floods fear with fullness, returning the ego to Mother's arms. The memory remains a ripple of awareness, but the debilitating emotion is merged into an ocean of bliss.

The healing that takes place through
Emotional QE is permanent.

How to Apply Emotional QE

First let your partner know that you do not have to know about his psychological pain. Explain that it is pure awareness that does the healing, and you only get the process started. He can keep his emotional discord private.

Ask him to think about the incident that is creating the distress. If there is no clear incident, then have him privately identify the emotion. Encourage him to allow his emotions to grow stronger. When they can get no stronger, ask him to grade his emotional discomfort on a scale from one to ten (ten being *unbearable*). Remember his pretest number.

Proceed as you did when removing physical problems with QE. (Refer back to Chapter 13 and reread the section called "Triangulation: The Three-Step QE Process.") First, find a tight or tender muscle for Contact A. Then find Contact B. Become acutely aware of contacts A and B, then both together. Wait for your Eufeeling to surface, and hold awareness of all three until you feel your partner's muscles relaxing under your touch.

When you have finished the session, give your partner some time to reorient. Emotional QE may sometimes require more time than QE applied to physical complaints. As soon as your partner is ready, have him bring up the same incident and once again assess its impact on a scale from one to ten.

At this point, partners usually express that they cannot even bring the emotion to mind! Or they will say something like: "I'm trying, but all I can get is a one or two." You can see that their facial muscles have relaxed, and there is serenity in their voice.

Emotional QE instantly removes uncomfortable emotions even when a person doesn't know why they are there. Pure awareness is able to get to the root without conscious awareness. On occasion, your partners may remember the offending event and mention it during the session. This is especially so when they discover a deeply buried childhood trauma. Don't put much emphasis on this. Ask them to remain silent and close their eyes if they like. The abhorrent emotion has already been neutralized by the time your partners have retrieved the memory, so there is no value in spending any more time on it.

You can feel content that you were able to inspire a healing of your partner's emotional conflict, and our troubled world is one candle brighter.

Emotional QE instantly removes uncomfortable emotions even when a person doesn't know why they are there.

CHAPTER 16

REMOTE QUANTUM ENTRAINMENT

"He who knows best knows how little he knows."

— THOMAS JEFFERSON

Another amazing fact about Quantum Entrainment is that you can perform it on someone without actually touching the person. You can do Remote QE from across a room or across the world. I recently had occasion to work with a partner named Eva who lived in Prague. As the crow flies, the Czech Republic is a considerable distance from my office in Sarasota, Florida. Eva, a student, was experiencing anxiety and always felt rushed.

We communicated through e-mail, and she wrote: "From the time I wake up till the time I fall asleep, I feel like I'm studying for a final exam." I never talked to Eva on the phone, nor did I know what she looked like. All I had were her words from an e-mail.

> *You can do Remote QE from across a room or across the world.*

Eva wanted relief from her constant anxiety. She desired a more directed energy to replace the hectic, erratic animation that defined her life. I performed Remote QE in the evening in Sarasota, which turned out to be around 4 A.M. in Prague. When I booted up my trusty ol' laptop the next morning, I was greeted by Eva's response. I include it here with only some minor grammatical edits, although maybe I should have taken out a few of the exclamation points.

Dear Frank,

I want to thank you so much for your help!!! I want to tell you that when I got up this morning, it was the first time since a long period I had the feeling "to own all the energy of the world." I mean I felt so much energy and power, and also when I was jogging this morning, I had a lot of positive thoughts and energy. So something changed, and I enjoyed and still enjoy it!!!!

Thank you!!!!

Hopefully you understand my English, it's not perfect ;-)

Dekuji mnohokrat ("Thank you very much"). And a lot of sunshine and greetings from Prague.

Eva

The entity that is Eva is made of the same stuff as the entity Frank. Pure awareness is not confined by time or space. It is everywhere, all of the time. It is only our limited conception, our *me*, that creates time and limits space. I inspired a healing event in the entity Eva by perceiving how we are the same, not how we are different. The sameness is pure awareness.

When you practice QE, you work from the level of ultimate sameness to effect healing changes in the world of differences.

*I inspired a healing event in the entity Eva by perceiving
how we are the same, not how we are different.*

In quantum physics, this instantaneous interaction at a distance is called *entanglement*. However, entanglement cannot transmit information faster than light. Whether the healing information that was transmitted to Eva was faster than the speed of light, I cannot say. It is a fascinating discussion but way outside the scope of this book. For our purposes here, it really doesn't matter. Somehow healing information found its way 5,000 miles to Eva's doorstep and didn't have to stop for directions on the way. That is good enough for me.

Tens of thousands of people around the world are performing QE on their friends, family members, and perfect strangers with great success just from reading the very book that you are holding in your hands. Many of those people have read these words translated into their own language, and QE still works. As a matter of convenience, most of those QE sessions are done remotely; and those initiators, as you will soon discover, were able to do QE with ease. If you find Remote QE impossible to believe, don't worry about it. You will still be able to do it no matter what you think is or isn't possible. Quantum Entrainment is a scientifically reproducible procedure. *It is real.* It does not need belief to work. And if you don't believe that, ask any pain-free pets if they were asked to believe in QE before they were healed.

*Quantum Entrainment is a scientifically reproducible
procedure. It is real. It does not need belief to work.*

How to Do Remote QE

To practice Remote QE, you will triangulate as you have in the other forms of Quantum Entrainment. The steps are the same with some minor adaptations. It's necessary to compensate for the lack of a physical partner, but Remote QE is infinitely easier to learn than other activities where you need a partner. For some obscure reason, the tango comes to mind. Oh well . . . here are a few suggestions.

Use a Surrogate

A surrogate is a replacement, someone who takes the place of your partner. Any warm body will do—your spouse or kids, the paperboy, the guy in the next cubicle. Just perform Remote QE on the physically present surrogate as if your absent partner were standing right in front of you. Make sure that your intention includes the name, image, or idea of your missing partner.

You can also use a pet as a surrogate. Animals usually make good stand-ins because they don't ask questions. They are used to the strange behavior of their masters and will probably submit willingly as long as there is a snack waiting for them at the end of the session. Although admittedly it may take quick fingers and a box of Band-Aids if your only pet is a ravenous piranha, the upside is that the snack would be provided during the QE session rather than afterward.

A third kind of surrogate can be a doll or stuffed animal. Actually, you could even draw a picture on a piece of paper and use that. Or just write down your partner's name. All of these replacements will work just fine. Give it a try, and you'll be pleasantly surprised.

Engage Your Imagination

If you have an active imagination, you can conjure up a mental image of your partner and triangulate in your mind's eye. Your fingers will not be touching anything, so you will have to visualize that, too. How do you know when to stop? You will feel the relaxation or melting sensation under your fingers just as you do when you're actually touching your partner.

Imagination QE can be done in a couple of ways. You can imagine that you are where your partner is. Visualize her sitting in her favorite chair while you apply Remote QE. Another option is to bring your partner to you. See her right there in front of you while you work your magic. Or you can meet anyplace you like. You are limited only by your imagination!

Try Air QE

You've heard of air guitar—pretending to hold the neck of an imaginary guitar while you pick, strum, and gyrate wildly in front of the mirror? Well, Air QE is a little like that. Imagine your partner in front of you standing or sitting. Whether your eyes are open or closed is completely up to you. Now physically move your body and reach out your hands to place your fingers on your absent partner. You do everything just as if your partner were there. Just don't let your spouse walk by unawares in the middle of the session. "Lucy, you got some splainin' to do!"

Remote QE is a wonderful way to get in all the QE practice you need. I do a session every night before I go to bed. I also include partners who need continued care with chronic or life-threatening illnesses like Alzheimer's and cancer.

Friends who at first thought regular Quantum Entrainment was weird now regularly call and ask for Remote QE.

My youngest daughter is a police officer in an economically depressed and crime-ridden city. She is always getting into a scuffle of one sort or another. I'm no longer surprised when I get a call from her saying, "Hey, Dad, I was putting a woman on PCP in the cruiser when she bit a chunk of flesh out of my leg. Could you QE me tonight?" or "I tore my shoulder up again in a foot pursuit. How about working on the pain and range of motion for me?" Ah, the joys of being a parent.

With practice, you will soon be able to conduct Remote QE anytime there is a break in your day. I've even done it while partners were describing their problem to me. By the time they finished their explanation, the pain had disappeared. It is absolutely wonderful to be so close to the creative force and watch it work its wonders. Our only limits are our unaware minds—and Quantum Entrainment will fix that, too.

How to Perform QE on Yourself

You already know how to work the marvels of Quantum Entrainment on yourself. Just pick a method already described and apply it to yourself. Of course, it helps to have the home edition of *Twister: For Double-Jointed Yoga Masters* if you want to physically work on your back or other hard-to-reach places. But remember, you don't have to contact the affected area. If you have mid-back pain, you can triangulate on your knee or chest and be equally effective. Also consider using one of the Remote QE techniques previously mentioned.

James, a QE practitioner, has found Remote QE very helpful in his practice of yoga. He explains how he does it:

"Since learning about Quantum Entrainment, I have used it on myself while practicing yoga. I find that I am going deeper into the asanas (poses), and going more quickly into stillness or still-point consciousness while practicing yoga. In place of using my hands to triangulate on my body, I use awareness to connect the three points. Then I just relax into pure awareness for a few seconds.

"Following this, my body seems refreshed, relaxed, and stronger. This application of Quantum Entrainment can be used in any situation, and can facilitate a shift in identification from limited body-mind consciousness to infinite pure awareness."

The potential for QE is limited only by your imagination. It is your nature to expand and grow. Put on your QE glasses and have a look around. Experiment and play with different ideas, but most of all have fun.

The potential for QE is limited only by your imagination.

Animals and Inanimate Objects

Because Quantum Entrainment draws from the most basic and all-permeating pure awareness, it should also work on animals and even inanimate objects. And it does! It's not all that strange when you think about it. We give medicines or chiropractic adjustments to our pets. But when it comes to so-called inanimate objects, I guess it is a bit of a stretch to think that we could pour a can of Red Bull into our depleted car battery to give it new life.

I say *so-called* inanimate objects because all of creation is vibrating with life on the subtlest level. Nothing is inanimate in the ultimate sense. And within the subtlest vibration exists its cause: pure awareness. So when it comes to a dead car battery, QE is cheaper than Red Bull and there is no can to recycle.

Nothing is inanimate in the ultimate sense.

One of our workshop graduates reported that he had a dead car battery. After making a number of unsuccessful attempts to start his car by turning the key in the ignition, he decided to try QE on the battery. The car kicked right over, and the engine purred to life. When he took the car into the shop, his mechanic said that the battery was indeed the culprit. He probably didn't mention to the mechanic that the jumper cables he used were his fingers.

Quantum Entrainment has universal influence and that includes household appliances. I love this story from a creative QEer:

> *"I wanted to share my experience with Quantum Entrainment after attending the workshop. I woke up Sunday really hungry. So I applied the QE to my hunger, and the hunger left, but I still decided to make myself a smoothie. Just when I was about to start blending the smoothie, the blender motor didn't work. It was completely dead. So I decided to apply QE to the blender. I worked with it for a few seconds . . . nothing at first. I tried again, this time completely letting go of a desired outcome. It worked! The blender was back to normal, and I got to enjoy my smoothie while being completely humbled by the experience. My roommate, who also loves smoothies, is amazed when I zap the blender before each use."*

Remember that your partner does not have to believe in this healing method to get results or even know that you're conducting it. Thus, as I've mentioned, animals respond beautifully to Quantum Entrainment. Apply QE to your pet's problems or even to pesky varmints such as overenthusiastic raccoons or bothersome bears.

Here's a case in point: A recent book signing for a bestselling author of alternative-healing books was held at a local yoga center. The air conditioners weren't working, and the doors had to be propped open. Uninterested in having their books signed, a dozen or so large black flies made a beeline for the huge pot of chicken soup on the snack table. Rob, the manager of the center, quickly ducked into the meditation room and "QE'ed" the little buggers. When he emerged a few minutes later, there was but a single fly buzzing around. And when the fly saw Rob materialize from the adjoining room, it promptly exited stage left.

Animals respond beautifully to Quantum Entrainment.

Food offers another area of exploration for creative QEers. Consider entraining your groceries, water, and nutritional supplements. Your intention might be to potentiate the beneficial ingredients or remove toxins, as well as to improve digestion and assimilation before a meal is eaten. If you say grace before a meal, then add Quantum Entrainment at the end of your prayer. In this way, the prayer becomes your intention, and QE takes that intention and lays it at the omnipresent feet of pure awareness.

CHAPTER 17

EXTENDED QUANTUM ENTRAINMENT

"Joy is not in things, it is in us."

— RICHARD WAGNER

Extended Quantum Entrainment is valuable for long-standing or life-threatening health concerns such as diabetes, heart disease, Alzheimer's, or cancer. It is also especially effective at soothing and healing deep emotional conflicts. When a malady does not respond after several minutes or several attempts of QE, then it is a candidate for Extended QE.

As the name implies, we are *extending* the usual time of QE, thus profoundly increasing the benefits to partner and initiator alike. When it is performed, the common world of cars, stars, people, and even space becomes supersaturated in the depths of pure awareness. So much so that pure awareness becomes almost tangible, a healing salve of vibrant renewal.

Extended Quantum Entrainment is valuable for long-standing or life-threatening health concerns.

Some years ago, when I was first developing Quantum Entrainment, I was invited to lunch by Mark, an acquaintance and fellow chiropractor. He said that he had a favor to ask, so when I arrived at the restaurant, I approached his table with some anticipation. When I looked into his normally energetic brown eyes, I saw a deep, sinking sadness. We greeted each other, exchanged pleasantries, and caught up on the doings of our colleagues.

Once we ordered our meals, Mark became pensive. He started to speak, halted, then looked down. I waited. He raised his head and tears had pooled in his eyes. I looked at him, encouraging him to continue with a nod of my head.

He began again, saying, "My wife has been fighting cancer for more than a year. She has fought hard, but yesterday she was admitted to the hospital. She has two malignant tumors. The one in her uterus is the size of a walnut, and the one in her liver is the size of a grapefruit. She is not expected to come home again.

"I know you do some kind of faith healing or meditation or something like that, and I was wondering if you could help Jillie."

I had never met his wife, but I agreed to go to the hospital that evening and visit her. I asked Mark to talk to the nursing staff to see if I could have an uninterrupted hour alone with Jillie. I also asked that no family be present during the last 60 minutes of visiting hours when I planned to arrive. He agreed. We finished our lunch in relative silence, and I returned to my afternoon patients.

That evening, I met Mark outside his wife's room. He told me that the nursing staff had been somewhat resistant to the idea of my doing anything *weird,* but they agreed to give us the time we needed. I paused outside her room, then pushed open the heavy door and walked into a dark and cheerless place.

The first thing I remember is the smell. It was not the smell of death but of the dying. I can't describe it, but it penetrates the mind and dampens the spirit. Jillie was asleep. She was a slight woman and her blonde hair lay tangled across her pillow. I didn't wake her, but I started Extended QE immediately.

Not five minutes later, a nurse came in to take Jillie's vitals and move a few things around and then left. Ten minutes later, she was back, and ten minutes after that someone else interrupted us for no apparent reason other than to make sure everything was in order. I thought I had inadvertently discovered a magical spell that could make nurses appear out of thin air in a busy hospital. I finished the hour with Jillie, who would wake occasionally only to fall back into a fitful sleep. Although Mark had told her I was coming, I didn't think she recognized me or was aware of my mission.

I returned the next night to pretty much the same routine from the staff, but Jillie was more alert and we had several brief exchanges throughout the hour. Despite the interruptions, I was able to hold pure awareness for most of the QE session. I left feeling lighter and somehow inspired.

When I arrived on the third night, there was a handwritten note on Jillie's door that said Do Not Enter, and it was signed by the head nurse on the evening shift. My first thought was that I was being ousted by a hostile staff fueled by ignorance about nonallopathic, *alternative* healing. I felt that this prejudice would be harmful to their patients and should not be tolerated. I marched over to the nurse's station and asked rather heatedly, "Why am I being kept from seeing Jillie?"

The answer shocked me. The nurse smiled kindly and said that the sign was for Jillie's and my benefit. It was put on the door so that we would not be disturbed. She told me that the nurses on all shifts had seen a remarkable change in Jillie's condition. They didn't know if what I was doing was the reason, but regardless, they assured me that my time in the room would be uninterrupted. And they were true to their word. It turns out that the prejudice was all mine.

I continued to perform Extended QE with Jillie every evening after seeing patients at my office. Her room eventually lost the feel and smell of death. She was more alert, and although we spoke infrequently in short, soft phrases, we started developing a nonverbal bond of inner knowing. The regular and sustained practice of quantum wakefulness had benefits for me as well. I found more peace and compassion growing in my life. I felt that I was blossoming somehow, awakening to a kind of immortality, free of the fear of death.

The morning after my eighth visit, I got a call from Mark. He told me that I didn't have to visit his wife in the hospital that evening because she was being released. He excitedly explained that the tumor in her uterus was gone, and the grapefruit-sized tumor in her liver was now the size of a walnut. I asked if he would like me to go to their home and continue with Extended QE, but he responded that Jillie wanted me to take some time off. She said that she could handle it from there.

Freed from her hospital bed, Jillie completely devoted her life to her family. I was invited to be a part of the family and attended a couple of their gatherings, but we gradually lost touch with each other. Over time, the cancer slowly returned. I offered to resume our QE sessions, but Jillie refused. Her words surprised me, but her voice told me that she was at peace. She quietly passed away at home, surrounded by her family. Mark later told me that Jillie believed that her "second life" was a godsend and her happiest time in this world.

Extended QE is remarkably powerful. And it is especially important to remember that pure awareness knows what needs to be done. Because it is human nature, we feel the need for stronger desire and more effort when working with life-threatening conditions. It is easy to forget that we are initiators with a simple intention, and that is all. Healing either will take place or it won't—that is out of our hands. The severity of the condition does not call for stronger intention or more effort. Simple innocence is called for, and nothing more.

Extended QE is remarkably powerful.

How to Do Extended QE

An Extended QE session can last from five minutes to an hour or so. Twenty minutes seems about right for most of my sessions, although I will lengthen or shorten the time as needed.

Begin an Extended QE session exactly as you would a regular QE session of one or two minutes. I like to start out standing and then have my partner sit down a couple of minutes later. Extended QE can also be done lying down, especially if your partner is ill.

There are some minor differences with Extended QE that should be noted. To start, hold your contact points and wait for your Eufeeling. Once you get the initial relaxation or dissolving sensation that signals the end of regular QE, continue to hold your Eufeeling. You can forget about being aware of your contact fingers, and simply focus on your Eufeeling. From time to time, your mind will wander, and when you realize that it's elsewhere, again become aware of your Eufeeling. Your original Eufeeling will more than likely change. You may first experience stillness or peace that may give way to bliss, joy, or even ecstasy. Whatever Eufeeling is there, just be aware of it.

Every few minutes, when the notion strikes you, move your contact fingers to other parts of your partner's body. Common places for Extended QE are the forehead, temples, heart, and solar plexus although any appropriate area of the body will do just fine. As soon as your fingers find their new position, return to your Eufeeling and settle in for the next few minutes.

During the lengthened session, you can occasionally re-state or rephrase your intention. This keeps your mind lively and on point. You might also naturally see your intention at work with your *inner vision*. You may perceive joints healing or lungs opening to receive life-giving air. You may see or feel other healing forces at work, too. Don't get involved. Whatever you view, just let it unfold on its own. You have a front-row seat as the healing impulses of pure awareness rise up and take form. You are the innocent observer to creation and re-creation. Nothing you do can improve on that. Know that this time is special, and you are blessed to be the silent witness.

You may also see geometric symbols or the flowing and swirling of abstract energies at work within you and your partner's body. The heavens may open and golden light may shine down upon you. Angels may sing and blow their trumpets to herald the coming healing. Your job? Just take it all in. Don't get caught up in the symbolism or symptom-atology of it all. Just be there and enjoy the ever-growing healing presence of pure awareness.

> *Know that this time is special, and you are*
> *blessed to be the silent witness.*

When the Extended QE session is over, allow at least two or three minutes for your partners to open their eyes and return to regular activities. That is a minimum. They may need a full five or ten minutes, or to even lie down afterward. Make sure to let them know that if they get tired later in the day, they should rest and should also get a good night's sleep.

As with the shorter QE sessions, the healing that is started during Extended QE will continue for a day or two afterward. On occasion, your partner may feel tired or emotional the following day. This is an indication that very deep healing is taking place, and, if at all possible, your partner should rest, eat well, and do some light exercises.

I rely heavily on Extended QE in my counseling practice. It is a remarkably potent purifier of emotions and healer of the body. And, of course, I love it for what it does for me. I will continue to rely on it until I experience that final paradigm shift that allows me to walk through walls or float featherlike through the air.

Until that happens—and I'll certainly let you know when it does—it's Quantum Entrainment in all its variations for me.

CHAPTER 18

USER-FRIENDLY WORLD PEACE

"Now there is one outstandingly important fact regarding Spaceship Earth, and that is that no instruction book came with it."

— BUCKMINSTER FULLER

I just want to take a few minutes to thank you for dropping by and spending this time with me. I am continually inspired by you and thousands of people like you who have opened their minds to the possibility of the impossible. I want Quantum Entrainment to work for you. I have QE'ed this book with that intention. I want you to be completely successful, and that is not entirely altruistic on my part. After all, every time you do QE, I benefit; indeed, the whole world benefits. If you don't see that now, you will soon.

My challenge, my plea to you, is simple: Practice QE and spread the healing power of pure awareness quickly and fully among your fellow human beings. You, being closest to the fire of awareness, will harvest the most benefit. But *everyone* will reap the rewards of your simple effort. And as more people perform Quantum Entrainment, they will each become more successful and fulfilled in every avenue of their lives. *As we think, so we live.*

"Thinking outside the box," a phrase I hope will soon fall into disuse, should be the norm. In fact, thinking based on boundlessness has to become commonplace to ensure the safety and sanity of our race. That humankind is struggling to survive is no news flash. We have been inching our way toward oblivion for generations. Each discordant thought we create is like one more grain of sand added to the quicksand that is slowly dragging us down. This, of course, is insanity. We all know insanity: doing the same thing over and over yet expecting different results. Our new world will not come from documents and proclamations. It cannot unfold out of the common and collective consciousness that has dominated human thought to this point. It will not come from outside, but from deep within where perfect awareness awaits.

> *Each discordant thought we create is like one more*
> *grain of sand added to the quicksand that*
> *is slowly dragging us down.*

Now I know it seems just a little grandiose to suggest that a simple healing process can save our collective bacon, but it can, for it is not the process, but the awareness we bring to the task, that wields the ultimate power. You have seen that for yourself. Awareness heals. The more you are aware, the more healing occurs in and around you. It does so naturally, spontaneously, and without effort.

We, collectively known as the human race, have but a single lesson to learn: Be aware. We are continually being reminded to *live in the present*. But what does that mean? Are we supposed to stop planning for the future or give up our memories? Of course not. Living in the *now* is living in pure awareness, which extinguishes psychological time—freeing the mind from the need "to do," and allowing it to reflect timeless and perfect order. An aware mind is organized, energetic, and creative. An aware mind is peaceful and can do no harm.

> *We, collectively known as the human race,*
> *have but a single lesson to learn: Be aware.*

Carl Jung's collective unconscious and, more recently, Rupert Sheldrake's "morphic field" illustrate a vital point about being human. As it turns out, we are not isolated entities aimlessly rambling around in a body-mind. We have an infinitely intimate relationship with every other soul on this planet. Every one of our thoughts and actions influences every other breathing being.

Thoughts are charged clouds that attract other thoughts of like charge. The more people think similar thoughts, the more momentum these clouds of consciousness gather. This is what Sheldrake calls a *morphic field*. Not only do we feed these morphic fields, but we are also influenced by them.

You can see that what you think and experience is very important. If you have ever wondered why people keep performing the same damaging behavior, you have your answer in the morphic field.

The most powerful, life-supporting morphic field is one created by individuals who are experiencing pure awareness. This brings us to my point about user-friendly world peace. Quantum Entrainment has enormous value as a healing procedure, but that is just the tip of the iceberg. When even a small percentage of people become clearly aware, it positively influences the minds and lives of everyone, even those who are not reflecting pure awareness. That's right—even as little as one percent of a population reflecting the coherency of pure awareness can have profound effects on the immediate surroundings, from there spreading to awaken the whole world. This is not some fanciful philosophy but scientific fact.

Beginning in the early 1960s, the Transcendental Meditation (TM) organization demonstrated the *one percent effect*. They were able to confirm that if only one percent of a city's population was experiencing the coherency of pure awareness, the crime rate would drop. To demonstrate, they would take a small number of TM practitioners into a city and, as a group, simply become aware. Using the FBI's crime statistics for 22 cities, the group was able to significantly reduce the overall crime rate by an average of 24 percent! Since then, there have been numerous other studies to show the ways in which focused awareness alone can change our lives for the better.

In her book *The Intention Experiment,* Lynne McTaggart presents a number of sound scientific studies that support this very point. She even gives us the number of aware people it would take to create a wave of coherency in the United States and the world. Are you ready for this? To immediately create a healthier, cleaner, and more loving life for all the inhabitants of the United States, it will take only 1,730 aware people. To have peace and prosperity spread throughout the world, just 8,084 people are needed to practice awareness. We literally have the technology to save the world right at our fingertips.

The Quantum Entrainment process has the power to heal your world locally, but that influence is not confined to just you and your immediate concerns. When you practice it, your soothing influence instantly radiates outward to help heal the ills of us all. I forget the name of the French philosopher who said that just the simple act of bending over and picking a flower changes the center of gravity of the entire universe. It's no different when you create a QE healing event. Every time you perform QE, you plant a seed that will produce a blossom of the greatest rarity. Like dropping a pebble in a quiet pond, your healing touch will send peaceful ripples that will gently rock the distant shores of every universe. Every time you create a QE healing event, you make the world a better place.

> *We literally have the technology to save the*
> *world right at our fingertips.*

Of course Quantum Entrainment is not the only way to awareness. There are thousands of roads to inner peace and outer harmony. I am making a plea for all of us to become more aware every day, as often as we can. QE is simple, instantaneous, and fun. It has immediate practical benefits as well as long-standing effects on the body, mind, and environment. It doesn't require that you set aside a time and place to practice. You can do it anytime, anywhere.

Additionally, this healing technique doesn't just ask you to sit in awareness. QE teaches you to move through that fullness, amplifying its profundity and quickly establishing it in your day-to-day life. These advantages make it the perfect practice for the monk, the mogul, or the single mother of three. Do QE throughout the day, every day. Do it by itself or add it to other self-awareness systems to increase their effectiveness. Add QE at the end of your meditations or prayers, during business meetings, while you are stuck in traffic, or while waiting in the "10 items or less" lane with your arms full of last-minute dinner items. Do this simple thing and witness firsthand a miraculous transformation that it will bring to your life.

If you don't believe that what I'm saying can possibly be true, then you must take the challenge. For if I am wrong, we humans have painted ourselves into a dreadfully bleak corner, and you have nothing to lose. Even so, you still have a pretty remarkable tool for healing sprains, indigestion, a broken heart, and the like. But if I am right, you will become one of the first to break into the light of a life of prosperity and peace. There is only one thing holding you back—a belief that it can't be so. The only belief that you have to overcome is the one stopping you from taking the first step. After that, it's easy. I'm reminded of a short discourse between Alice and the White Queen from Lewis Carroll's *Through the Looking-Glass:*

> "There's no use trying," [Alice] said: "one *can't* believe impossible things."
>
> "I daresay you haven't had much practice," said the Queen. "When I was your age, I always did it for half-an-hour a day. Why, sometimes I've believed as many as six impossible things before breakfast."

I am not even asking you to change your beliefs. Beliefs don't change the world—awareness does. So keep your beliefs intact if you wish, but be aware. Awareness will allow you to keep those beliefs that work and will softly dissolve the ones that don't simultaneously serve you and others.

Practice Quantum Entrainment often and maintain a playful sense of purpose. Become a child exploring your surroundings for the first time, with your eyes wide open. When was the last time, in this feverish world, you gave in to the magic of the moment? Do you remember the joy of lying on your back in the grass while watching clouds slide lazily across a deep blue sky? You may not have recognized then the pure awareness that spawned in you the profound sense of peace and joy, but now that you know pure awareness, let it enfold you completely in its arms.

Help yourself to what is already yours. Heal your world, and thereby heal our world, one soul at a time.

ABOUT THE
AUTHOR

Dr. Frank J. Kinslow has been researching and teaching
healing techniques for more than 35 years. He draws from
his clinical experience as a chiropractic physician, in-depth
studies into Eastern esoteric philosophies and practices, and
an ardent love of relativity and quantum physics. In 2007,
the Quantum Entrainment® process of instant healing was
born out of a personal crisis that left Dr. Kinslow with *nowhere to go and nothing to do.* Out of this *nothing,* he was able
to create a vibrant and fulfilling life for himself. He began to
teach and write with such simplicity and clarity that in just
a few years, tens of thousands of people around the world
were able to create vibrant and fulfilling lives for themselves
just by reading his books.

Dr. Kinslow is a chiropractic physician, a teacher for the
deaf, and a Doctor of Clinical Spiritual Counseling. He continues to write and teach extensively. He resides in Sarasota,
Florida, with his wife, Martina.Listen for Dr. Kinslow on
HayHouseRadio.com.

Website: **www.QuantumEntrainment.com**

ABOUT THE QE ORGANIZATION

Dr. Kinslow is the originator and sole teacher of Quantum Entrainment®. He conducts seminars and lectures worldwide. He is training Certified QE Practitioners who are qualified to give QE healing sessions in a clinical setting. To schedule a session with a Certified QE Practitioner, go to the Products/Services page on the QE website. For more information about QE, please contact the organization:

Website: **www.QuantumEntrainment.com**
E-mail: **info@QuantumEntrainment.com**
Phone: (877) 811-5287 (toll-free in North America)

QE Products

Books

> *The Secret of Quantum Living*
> *Eufeeling! The Art of Creating Inner Peace and Outer Prosperity*
> *Beyond Happiness*

Audio Books

> *The Secret of Instant Healing*
> *The Secret of Quantum Living*
> *Beyond Happiness*

CDs

> *Exercises for Quantum Living* (2-CD set)
> *Exercises for Quantum Living for Two* (2-CD set)
> *Quantum Entrainment Exercises*

DVDs

> *What the Bleep QE Video*
> *Introduction to Quantum Entrainment*

Other Services Found at
www.QuantumEntrainment.com:

- Certified QE Practitioner Sessions
- The QE Quill Newsletter
- Free Downloads
- QE Videos
- QE Forum

Hay House Titles of Related Interest

YOU CAN HEAL YOUR LIFE, the movie,
starring Louise L. Hay & Friends
(available as a 1-DVD program and an expanded 2-DVD set)
Watch the trailer at: **www.LouiseHayMovie.com**

THE SHIFT, the movie, starring Dr. Wayne W. Dyer
(available as a 1-DVD program and an expanded 2-DVD set)
Watch the trailer at: **www.DyerMovie.com**

∾

THE AMAZING POWER OF DELIBERATE INTENT:
Living the Art of Allowing, by Esther and Jerry Hicks
(The Teachings of Abraham®)

THE BODY "KNOWS": How to Tune In to Your Body
and Improve Your Health, by Caroline Sutherland

DEFY GRAVITY: Healing Beyond the Bounds of Reason,
by Caroline Myss

INSIDE-OUT HEALING: Transforming Your Life Through
the Power of Presence, by Richard Moss

THE RECONNECTION: Heal Others, Heal Yourself,
by Dr. Eric Pearl

TRANSCENDENTAL MEDITATION: The Essential Teachings of
Maharishi Mahesh Yogi. Revised and Updated for the
21st Century, by Jack Forem (available October 2011)

UNLOCK THE SECRET MESSAGES OF YOUR BODY!
A 28-Day Jump-Start Program for Radiant Health
and Glorious Vitality, by Denise Linn

All of the above are available at your local bookstore,
or may be ordered by contacting Hay House (see next page).

~

We hope you enjoyed this Hay House book. If you'd like to receive
our online catalog featuring additional information on
Hay House books and products, or if you'd like to find
out more about the Hay Foundation, please contact:

Hay House, Inc.
P.O. Box 5100
Carlsbad, CA 92018-5100
(760) 431-7695 or **(800) 654-5126**
(760) 431-6948 (fax) or **(800) 650-5115 (fax)**
www.hayhouse.com® • **www.hayfoundation.org**

~

Published and distributed in Australia by: Hay House Australia
Pty. Ltd., 18/36 Ralph St., Alexandria NSW 2015 • *Phone:* 612-9669-4299
Fax: 612-9669-4144 • www.hayhouse.com.au

Published and distributed in the United Kingdom by: Hay House UK, Ltd.,
292B Kensal Rd., London W10 5BE • *Phone:* 44-20-8962-1230
Fax: 44-20-8962-1239 • www.hayhouse.co.uk

Published and distributed in the Republic of South Africa by: Hay House SA
(Pty), Ltd., P.O. Box 990, Witkoppen 2068 • *Phone/Fax:* 27-11-467-8904
info@hayhouse.co.za • www.hayhouse.co.za

Published in India by: Hay House Publishers India, Muskaan Complex,
Plot No. 3, B-2, Vasant Kunj, New Delhi 110 070 • *Phone:* 91-11-4176-1620
Fax: 91-11-4176-1630 • www.hayhouse.co.in

Distributed in Canada by: Raincoast, 9050 Shaughnessy St.,
Vancouver, B.C. • V6P 6E5 • *Phone:* (604) 323-7100
Fax: (604) 323-2600 • www.raincoast.com

~

Take Your Soul on a Vacation

Visit **www.HealYourLife.com**® to regroup, recharge, and reconnect
with your own magnificence.Featuring blogs, mind-body-spirit news,
and life-changing wisdom from Louise Hay and friends.

Visit **www.HealYourLife.com** today!